Along
the
Ganges

To
Prof. S.A. Upadhyayaji and Mataji
with gratitude and love

Along
the
Ganges

Ilija Trojanow

Translated from the German
by the author with Ranjit Hoskote

 ArmchairTraveller

HAUS PUBLISHING
London

First published in Germany as *An den inneren Ufern Indiens* by
Carl Hanser Verlag, 2003
First published in India by Penguin Books India 2005
Copyright © Ilija Trojanow 2005

This English translation first published in Great Britain in 2005 by
Haus Publishing Limited, 26 Cadogan Court, Draycott Avenue,
London SW3 3BX

The moral rights of the authors have been asserted.
A CIP catalogue record for this book is available from the British
Library
ISBN 1-904950-36-1

Designed and typeset in Garamond by Andrea El-Akshar, Köln
Printed and bound by Graphicom in Vicenza, Italy
Jacket illustration: Getty Images

Contents

Drops from
the
Locks of God

The man pulls the goat into the Ganges until the water slaps against its belly. With wet hands he strokes her swollen womb. He splashes water on her, whispers in her ear. Then he leads her out of the water and as soon as she feels solid ground beneath her hooves, she throws: two kids. The shepherd cuts the navel cord, takes the newborn into his arms and sets out for his village nearby. The river flows on, unhurried; with measured brush strokes ferrymen cover the keels of their boats with tar. Two sadhus fill their lotas and greet us in god's name. A few cows lap up water. The birth seems as casual as the buzz of a fly, the calloused skin on the heel of a fisherman. It leaves nothing behind besides a cord, carelessly thrown away, and the memory of one further severing of the umbilical cord.

3

Not everything is born this quietly. *Ganga* bursts out of the glacier and, with a long-drawn shout, falls to the earth, and then off she goes, impetuous, head over heels. She takes hold of *Shiva*'s head—hard on impact, soft when she flows off. She falls, beads on his forehead, pearls from his locks—her stormy roar, his starry silence—right into the last furrow of his face. The cascades shake him out of his self-absorption. He can no longer remain still, he jumps up and rattles his *damru*. It sounds like splitting ice, endlessly splitting, until it consists of nothing but drops that fall from his lips. *Ganga* grasps *Shiva*'s hands, the two begin to whirl around the melting moment. The beat of many drops becomes a torrent. The maelstrom swallows all, the echo of oblivion, the sleeping rocks, the two horns that rise above the glacier which looks like the wrinkled face of an old and revered cow.

'Not so fast,' a breathless *Ganga* whispers.

'Faster,' a raring *Shiva* shouts.

And they whirl on.

For hours the ecstasy of this birth had kept me awake, my own head throbbing with pain. Early in the morning we had left Gangotri, walking twenty kilometres, climbing a thousand metres. We had reached the glacier, Gaumukh, shortly before sunset. In our hurry we had pitched our tent too close to the river. My companion Pac, an enchanting photographer, whose eyes during our journey passed through every shade of green and brown, was fast asleep, undisturbed by the relentless roar. The mouth of the glacier was just a few hundred metres away. I thought I heard the glacier groan—we were two insomniacs sharing a long night. I stepped out of the tent, into the cold of high altitude. Shining ice blocks floated by. The torrents pummelled the rocks. In the midst of the whirlpool, *Shiva* danced—like a shaman in a trance, like a medicine man conjuring fertility—his dance of creation and cessation. The first sounds rolled out of his *damru*: the smacking lips of a *pujari*, the ringing bells of the *mandir* in Gangotri, the flutter of the saf-fron flags on mountain bikes, the hooting buses in Uttarkashi, the rattle of the bulldozers in Tehri, the

5

high-pitched loudspeakers at Triveni *Ghat*, the *bols* of a *tabla pandit*. *Shiva*'s heart beat *da da da*. With every whirl he crowned himself with froth and threw another sound at the world, until the roar dissolved into uncountable sounds and tones.

The morning after the sleepless night, my head felt like a kite with its string cut. The front of the glacier glowed turquoise, a faded amethyst. The ice was covered with debris; it humped under the weight of constant change. In the last twenty years the glacier has withdrawn more than one kilometre. No other glacier in the world shrinks as rapidly as this. The other fifteen thousand glaciers in the Himalayas are all thawing, as if mankind had left the freezer open. Scientists from the Jawaharlal Nehru University in Delhi have warned that many of these glaciers could disappear by the year 2035, their downfall followed by floods and then by droughts. The *pujari* would hardly have been surprised by this prediction. The *Brahmavaivarta Purana* foretells that the Ganges will one day, when she has taken her share of sins, go underground in order to safeguard

6

her purity, awaiting the next golden age. The scientists blame global warming; the *pujari* would probably have referred to the dark ages, the *Kali Yuga*, that we live in. Once the cosmos is completely polluted and out of balance, the cycle of change will have to start anew. Both explanations complement one another on a broad canvas of human misdemeanour.

Our ill-advised wanderings ended abruptly as two mountaineers implored us to turn back immediately, since the glacier in the rainy season was as unsafe as an eroding slope. A cascade of stones behind our back echoed the warning. Stones tumbled into the valley, smaller than the sound they were making. The source was indiscernible until we glimpsed, high up on a steep face, two mountain antelopes nimbly leaping further up. The road to the other side of the river being blocked, we had to turn back and clamber over rocks to get closer to the chasm. Manu, our porter, meanwhile, protested loudly, invoking the memory of eleven pilgrims who had recently lost their lives when they were hit by rocks during their ritual *snaan*. When we had rounded the last bend, a wall of ice blocked our way. We gave up our hunt for insight, sat down and watched a *sadhu* strip right down to his red *langoti*, check the depth of the water with his stick and then slip into the river, as if into a bathtub, surrounded by ice floes. After his *snaan*, the meagre man rubbed himself with ash; not a goose pimple on him. Evidently no friend of small talk, he answered my question whether the water was not too cold for him with a silent nod.

We sat in front of Gaumukh for a long time, as though before a wonder.

Rampratap said, 'I want your jacket.'

'My jacket?'

'I am feeling cold.'

I shook my head.

Rampratap said, 'I want your watch.'

'What for? What does it matter in Gaumukh whether it is quarter to or quarter past five?'

He laughed indulgently. Our conversation seemed to run along traditional lines. I was the *raja* who had to give the priest a gift. He had no other source of income. So he tried to goad me into performing an expensive ritual, and it took a while before he was contented with a *puja* for Rs 501. We gave him the names of the friends on whose behalf he should perform the *puja*. He would start at three in the afternoon and go on for three hours at least, he professed in the tone of a supplier whose reliability was being questioned. He served us tea and made further enquiries into our procreative plans. We dumped his *chai* and started our journey back into the valley.

Sometimes people mistake a mountain for *Shiva* and call it Shivling. A group of Koreans had tried to climb the peak. They had put up their base camp near Tapovan, where two sadhus and a woman convert from Israel spend each summer in god's vicinity. The mountaineers had to abort their mission just two hundred metres below the peak. They now beat a retreat, crushed losers. The beauty of the glacier was lost on them: on their way up, they hadn't had the time to enjoy it, and, on the way down, they were not in the mood.

9

A map on a river-rock

The path clung to the northern slope of a deep and
narrow valley, a hundred metres above the river. The
water tumbled down, paused, freed itself, tumbled,
paused, freed itself, a harmonium that accompanied
a hoarse and fervent *bhajan*. Torrents crashed deeply
into the Ganges, blue and full of hope, and were
immediately sucked in by the roiling brown below.

The Ganges carries more sludge than any other
river in the world. Along with the Brahmaputra, it
erodes soil from the Himalayas in order to reclaim
land in the Bay of Bengal. The entire system of rivers
annually transports 2.9b mt of sediment downstream—the equivalent of 400 million truckloads.

An evenly formed rectangular block of stone
obstructed half of the river. A multitude of pebbles, in
the unassuming colours of the mountains, lay on it—a
stone garden laid out with every new flooding. Several
veins were marked on the visible side, like rivers on a
topographical map. The upper third of the block was
white; below it, beige. The boundary between wetness
and dryness was fringed by individual sprays.

We had been on the road just two hours when Manu heaved down the MacPac rucksack from his shoulders and took a short break. When I'd hired him, he had given me the impression that he could carry the burden of the world at a trot to every peak, but on the very first day his frequent complaints had forced me to strap on the rucksack myself. Manu was a local porter but his interests, his preferences, as well as his fashionable leather jacket, bespoke a certain alienation. He came from the village of Bhoki that lies above Gagnani, a health resort. He had finished school, which was eight steep kilometres away, at the age of twenty. After school, the whole valley lay at the feet of the privileged few. They moved, for further studies, to *Rishikesh* or Dehra Dun. A friend of his had even gone as far as Mumbai (formerly Bombay), to Borivli— the knowledge of the name of this suburb made the Fata Morgana Mumbai appear a little more real. But Manu had had to stay back in Bhoki. His father had passed away two years ago and he, as the eldest son, had had to assume responsibility for the family which possessed a bit of land and a few apple trees.

He sometimes helped a friend of his father's at harvest-time; there was nothing else to do in the village. At the age of twenty-two, Manu seemed somehow to have reconciled himself to his life. He didn't appear unhappy, but a part of him seemed to sense that he was trapped for the rest of his life in an activity that he even now found boring.

We met a *sadhu* whose belongings included a small sack and a makeshift instrument, its resonance box wrapped in a plastic bag. In answer to my 'where-from, where-to?', he began to sing, '*Sita Ram Sita Ram, Sita Ram Ram Ram.*'

Shiva sat on a peak and meditated. While he withdrew from the world, *Taraka* visited terror upon it. The demon lusted to enslave all beings. Opposition was futile, for it only strengthened him. The mortal gods sought the help of *Brahma*, who had created this demon.

'I cannot undo what I have created.' To state such self-evident truths was *Brahma*'s discouraging privilege.

'Couldn't you at least give us a hint how to over-power him?' the mortal gods begged.

'I'll let you in on a secret,' *Brahma* said, more than a little tickled at the thought of the coming *tamasha*. '*Shiva*'s son could destroy *Taraka*.'

The anguish of the mortal gods echoed through all three worlds. The situation was hopeless. *Shiva* had no son; to make matters worse, he had just sunk into a deep meditation, and *Shiva*'s meditations were known to last for a whole age. It was unthinkable to disturb the Lord of Hermits. Dejected, the gods took leave of *Brahma*.

'One should not send guests away empty-handed.'

They froze in their tracks.

'There is one person who can entice *Shiva*. Her name is *Parvati*; her father is Himavat, the king of the Himalayas, her mother is the noble Mena.'

The mortal gods immediately hatched a plot. They roped in Kama, who brought about spring before its time. He had sown passion so often, had so often changed the course of emotions that he was all too sure of his irresistibility. When the virgin *Parvati* stood in front of *Shiva*, *Kama* drew an arrow from his quiver. He caressed its tip with his fingers and smiled lasciviously. *Parvati*'s breasts pressed against her blouse. The sari fell diagonally across her body, revealing a navel that was more beautiful than a lotus. *Kama* took aim with all the poise of a master archer. *Parvati* stepped closer, her hands folded in a gesture of innocent reverence, her body full of devotion. The arrow flew from the bow and struck where it was meant to strike. Anyone else would have succumbed immediately to *Parvati*'s charms, but not *Shiva*. He opened his third eye and reduced *Kama* to a heap of ashes. The wind flew into a rage and blew the ashes away. They settled in a field of roses, melted into the sweat of a bull, were picked up by the beak of a koel.

Parvati ran away. She withdrew into herself. It was as if the last of Kama's arrows had hit her. She could not banish *Shiva* from her thoughts. She kept repeating his name. She climbed up to Mount *Kailash* where he continued to fast and meditate. She caressed his stone body without touching it. She thought her way into his being. She felt incomplete without him.

One day, as she was standing in front of him, murmuring his name, she mispronounced it without noticing. Instead of '*Shiva*', the words *Shivo ham* (I am *Shiva*) escaped her lips. His eyes opened. It was spring again. The numbed heart began to pound—*da da ti re ki ta*. *Shiva* saw the valley, heard the chirping of birds, smelt fragrances that he had not known before. *Da da ti re ki ta*. And everything was infused with a whiff of the woman who stood in front of him and murmured 'Shivo ham'. Three syllables. And from the third, the additional one, arose the first embrace that lasted centuries.

Later, *Parvati* sat on his left lap. She looked up to him and asked, 'Who are you?'

Shiva replied, 'The entire world changes but I do not change. I cannot come into being because I have always been.'

'And who am I?'

'You are the creator, the mother of all mothers,' said *Shiva*. 'Nothing can exist without you.'

Parvati was saddened. 'What is left for me to do?'

'You are the only one who can narrate the world.'

And *Shiva* embraced her from behind so that he could see beyond her into the valley and across all peaks.

'This is the world. It lives and yet again it does not live, because nobody has ever told its story.'

His wild locks tickled her ears.

'Would you do that for me?'

'What should I do for you?'

'Narrate the world.'

The barrel weighed at least twenty kilos. It stood at the edge of the path, its carry-straps like sweat-soaked whips. The boy sitting next to it was not more than ten years old. He was shivering, his hands icy. There was water in the barrel, but the boy with the pretty face didn't know why he had to carry it. His smile was tense. He was exhausted and evidently disconcerted by our interest. Manu sat beside him and stroked his hands. 'He is one of us,' he said, although the boy came from Nepal. His parents had taken him out of school and handed him over to an uncle, who had sent him here two months ago. 'Because of money,' said Manu, helpfully.

The boy had been on the road for days, without documents, all alone. Now he carried the Ganges water from the source to Gangotri where it would be loaded on to trucks, jeeps and buses to be distributed across the country and to every corner of the world where Hindus live. During the ritual bath, a few drops of it are sprinkled on the idols or the human body. This water would be stored away safely, rationed, used only for special occasions, at important festivals like *Diwali* or *Durga Puja*. But the boy knew nothing of this. He was exhausted, the Ganges water a back-breaking burden.

The flooded tent

The *Devganga*, a small tributary, lies in the gigantic river course like a dwarf in a king-size bed. The previous night the dwarf had run amok, twisting and turning in the bed, flailing about like a drunk. On both banks, stones were cast up in heaps, traces of his fit of fury.

Padaman Singh had yet to forgive the mountain stream. The shopkeeper squatted among the ruins of his tented *dukan*.

At five in the morning, the rivulet had attacked him. Water had flowed all around him, black and cold. Springing from his cot, he had sunk almost knee-deep in water. Stones had struck against his ankles, against his shins. Padaman had run up a path, anything to get away, abandoning all thought of his stock. In the morning he inspected the night's accumulated debts. The river had washed away half of his goods, worth at least Rs 25,000. The rest had been saved by the piled-up rocks. He blamed the river for his misfortune, speaking of the night in the tone of a disappointed friend who could not fathom why he had been so shamefully betrayed.

He had done his best to rearrange the salvaged goods—crushed Tetra Paks of juice, mud-crusted cans of Thums-Up, soiled bottles of mineral water. A Coca-Cola crate turned upside down served as a pedestal, flattened tins of vegetable oil as trays. The structure was fortified by a large carton of Maggi two-minute noodles. The cardboard shelf contained a few plastic jars full of bubblegum and other types of chewing gum, a dozen cigarette packets, a few packets of biscuits and a few bars of chocolate. He was rebuilding his shop on its old site.

On the way up, we had managed to cross the *Devganga*, but now no ford could be discerned, no trunk lay at hand. The current ran strong and fast. Manu tried, with the heavy rucksack on his back, to find a reasonably safe way across the ice-cold waters, but slipped, and for a moment neither Manu nor the rucksack could be seen, before they popped up again, injured and dented. While I attended to Manu, a small band of pilgrims gathered on the bank, none too happy with Padaman Singh's moody statement that they would have to camp here till the waters receded.

'Overnight?'

'Oh, of course. Perhaps even a couple of days.'

Amongst those waiting was an Indian wearing the loud uniform of the *NRI*: Bermudas, sneakers, college T-shirt and baseball cap. He was accompanied by a chubby Canadian of Lebanese origin, a French yoga teacher who refreshed her knowledge every year in the Himalayas, and a blonde female with a sibylline smile whose origins remained a secret.

'Let's cross,' said the Indian American in the forceful tone of one who believes himself to be in control of his life. The disappointment of not making it across, despite his high-tech hiking stick, rattled him so badly that from then on he held aloof from the group, his gaze fixed on the ground as though he were a passionate entomologist.

All those who tried to make the crossing had to give up; hours later a few ponies appeared, their riders leading them through the currents without hesitation. The ponies sank in neck-deep, but eventually found a footing and their way across with loud neighs. The riders followed on foot, hopping across the flood like frogs. They could read the river; they knew they had to set their feet down where the water was broiling, where the agitated surface spoke of a stone that had been washed under. When they reached the other side, one of them, a very good-looking man with an overflowing moustache, stepped into the water again, staged a calm crossing, presented himself before Pac, and offered gallantly to carry her across. The others were not accorded even a glance. Pac suggested that he should first prove himself with me. So the four horsemen formed a chain and I was passed on from one to the other, every step of mine accompanied by shouted directions as to where to place my foot, mostly where it seemed especially dangerous. Drenched but unhurt, I finally made it to the other shore. Next came the Canadian—the yellow Polo T-shirt bobbed along the water like a buoy— then Pac was conveyed across, and the pony-drivers began to take their heartfelt leave of her. At this the Canadian panicked. Fishing out his wallet, he thrust a wad of wet currency notes at Mohan, our providential helper.

'Money, I will give you money. How much money?'

'No,' protested Mohan, 'no money,' and turned away.

I explained to him that we were all members of one group and had therefore to stay together. Thus beseeched, the men continued the rescue operation. The other travellers were also eager to express their gratitude, in wet currency, as soon as they felt the shore beneath their feet. Mohan's resistance finally crumbled: succumbing to the commercialization of helping thy neighbour, he asked one of his colleagues to start collecting the money.

When everyone had crossed the river, the rescuers queued up at our little first-aid box and let themselves be bandaged. Mohan pointed to a pus-swollen wound on his finger. All his heroics fell apart when he saw me wielding a needle and pincers. In a torrent of words, he refused even to be pricked. At the next tented shop, the men invited us to *chai*. They revelled in the pose of hardy pioneers; they cultivated a tone of gruff camaraderie. Several times a week, they climbed from Gangotri to Gaumukh, loaded or unloaded there, and led their ponies back into the valley. 'Hard work, good money.' The daily wage of Rs 600 was handsome, but the work was seasonal. And in winter, in the four long months of snow, what did they do then? They laughed: 'Sleeping, eating, sleeping, eating.'

Parvati and *Ganga* are sisters. Jealousy among siblings weighs heavy. While meditating, *Parvati* could forget everything but her sister. Every time *Parvati* looked up at her Lord, she saw *Ganga* bathing his hair, playing

22

hide-and-seek in the forest of his abundant locks. She envied her sister her fairer, more beautiful skin. She envied her the exciting life she led. One day the mortal gods had appeared and prevailed upon her father to let them take *Ganga* with them. They claimed that she was destined to flow as the Milky Way through the cosmos. Little *Parvati*, on the other hand, had to bear the monotonous existence of a princess in the palace of Himavat. And now she had to share even *Shiva* with her sister. She saw how a drop fell from his brow on to his lower lip. *Shiva*'s tongue savoured the drop lustfully as if it were a raisin. If only she were to become pregnant. But *Shiva* did not grant her this heart's desire. He was too distracted.

The road ends in Gangotri. Parts of this small town are concreted over with ugliness. A little *Shiva* stands caged, looking forlorn behind gigantic bars like a prisoner arrested on false charges. Ten steps lead to his cell. In front of it—the result of an official attempt to provide comfort to the pilgrims—are posted four benches, two on either side of the cleanly swept path that is occasionally sprayed by the foam of the nearby waterfall. In the middle of Gangotri, the Ganges dives twenty metres deep. The impact has polished smooth sculptures from the rocks. Until not so long ago, the glacier had stretched all the way down to this waterfall.

Pilgrims bathed dangerously close to the rapacious waters. The river rushed forward, the waves overtook each other; hectic as cars on an Indian road, they collided, they jetted up in fountains, struck against stones and washed the feet of a shivering, fragile man. He seemed to consist only of bone and callus; marked by a life of submission, he stepped aside with his head lowered. He allowed a *pujari*, who handled all details of ritual with the resolution of a sergeant major, to order him around. The pilgrims around the old man huddled together, reassuring themselves of their solidarity, while they stood quivering and insecure on the banks of the Ganges.

Behind the bathing *ghat* was a small house, 'Record Room' written above its entrance. The door was half open, like a mumbled invitation. I entered a room full of boxes, boxes made of wood and metal, in various colours and of different sizes, strewn around at random like the luggage of vanished travellers. A man was sitting on one of the boxes, his *dhoti* rucked up, his answers oblique and difficult to understand. The boxes contained ledgers, manuscript rolls, notebooks—entries spanning more than a hundred years. The local histories of pilgrimages, a chronology of hopes cooled along, blessings prayed for. This documentation centre holds the name of a pilgrim, his origins, his *gotra*, the *puja* he desires to perform and the date of his petition; and the man with the skinny legs and clean-shaven head was the archivist. His family has belonged to this holy place for generations; it has looked after the pilgrims and administered this library of boxes. In the old days, his family used to provide lodging to the pilgrims who were taken care of like relatives, against payment, of course. Over the generations, there developed a strong relationship between the pujaris and the pilgrim families.

'How come you are not dedicating a *puja*,' the man holds out a bait, 'so that one day we can tell your son exactly when you were here? I will be gone one day, but the files shall remain forever!' He presented me with his visiting card, which carried his telephone number, the blessing 'Victory to Ganges', as well as the names of his three 'suns'.

Next morning, when we were taking leave of Gangotri, everyone had gathered at the bus station. Mohan sat in a restaurant with his colleagues and played cards. The boy from Nepal grinned at us and did not leave our side. Manu sauntered along; he was waiting for the next bus. With the money he had earned, he could afford to go home for a few days. The Nepali boy was carrying Pac's camera bag while we negotiated the taxi price. When I asked the people around why the boy had to carry the heavy barrels filled with Ganges water, a Kashmiri counselled me in excellent English: If I was so concerned about his well-being, I should take him with me to my affluent country.

Encounters with deepak

On Limchgad Bridge, inaugurated on 30 June 2001, there was written in mighty letters: SNOW-CLAD MOUNTAINS, SCORCHING DESERTS, INACCESSIBLE POCKETS, B.R.O. IS SEEN EVERYWHERE. Behind the bridge the acronym was explained on a board: BORDER ROADS ORGANIZATION MAKE A WAY FOR YOUR BRIGHT FUTURE. Both sentences were signed by Deepak. It took me a few bends to understand that Deepak was the pen-name of an artistic soul who suffered neither creative cramps nor lack of ideas. Although he had committed a few mistakes typical of a beginner—too many adjectives, the idiom overwrought, striving but not arriving—Deepak was to gain in poetic stature as we descended from the mountain.

⁓

The gods, the human beings and the demons approached *Shiva* and asked him the right way to live. He closed his eyes and aeons passed.

Then they heard something, *da da da*, and they were not certain whether he had murmured something or whether they had sensed his heartbeat.

27

Shiva said nothing.

The gods begged him to speak to them. 'Da!' said *Shiva*. 'Did you understand?'

The gods thought, and thought, and said, 'We have understood you. You have pointed us to *dama*, to self-control.'

Then the human beings begged *Shiva* to speak to them. 'Da!' said *Shiva*. 'Did you understand?'

The human beings thought, and thought, and said, 'We have understood you. You have pointed us to *dana*, to solidarity.'

Then the demons begged *Shiva* to speak to them. 'Da!' said *Shiva*. 'Did you understand?'

The demons thought, and thought, and said, 'We have understood you. You have pointed us to *daya*, to forgiveness.'

Da da da like *dama*, like *dana*, like *daya*.

The gods, the human beings and the demons climbed down into the valley of life.

～

LIVE FOR TODAY, DRIVE FOR TOMORROW. Deepak made good use of advertising jargon. Provoked by the

80,000 victims of traffic accidents in India every year, he linked popular form with didactic content: ACCIDENTS BREED WHEN YOU OVERSPEED. His suggestions were painted in yellow brush strokes on dark rocks, in white letters on blue boards, in slightly scruffy handwriting or in pedantic capital letters; once in a while he ventured into Hindi and Devanagari. KEEP YOUR NERVE ON A SHARP CURVE. Once Deepak had discovered rhyme, he rarely forsook it. MOUNTAINS ARE A PLEASURE ONLY IF YOU DRIVE WITH LEISURE.

~

In Gangnani, where the river makes a steep curve, there was a small restaurant on piles that offered the usual fare of fried samosas and biscuits. Bollywood songs formed a swinging bridge across the Ganges. From the veranda of the restaurant, one could touch the tips of a tree that had grown up along the slope. A tattered piece of brown cloth was wrapped around a few of its buds, a blue plastic sheet was draped around its main trunk like a scarf and a rubber sandal balanced itself on the topmost branches, the soles facing the sky.

From Gangnani downwards the landscape was tranched into small terraced fields, like saris laid out to dry, in all shades of the green of blossoming rice. The sweat of hard work had seeped into the groundwater. On the windowless wall of a house facing the road, a naturalistically painted woman plucked tea, the ropes of her basket forming a headband. The soil and the people have been equally colonized by order.

The valley sank into a cloud of dust. Rice green was broken up by huge shovels. The slopes were devoid of trees, naked. Welcome to civilization—the demon *Taraka* screamed from the exhaust pipes of the trucks, dredgers and caterpillar tractors. He smirked, 'And you thought you would recover your image at the source of the Ganges. Actually, it is carved out of the mountains every day, your ugly face. There were times when this land was called Devbhumi, there were times when it really was the Land of the Gods. Now it belongs to you and me.' *Taraka* fell silent and a reservoir wall came into sight.

Tehri was a small mountain town, its antiquity apparent. The public spaces were narrow, the buildings characterized by the improvization of centuries. The town was cradled by a river that was no longer there. The canals of the dam were ready, the water had been diverted. Clocktower, palace, court stood as mute objections. It was evident that the town had been under a death sentence for many years. Many of the 4,551 registered families had already been 'rehabilitated', a euphemism for uprooting the residents from familiar surroundings without offering them viable alternatives. Some of them had been moved to New Tehri, less than twenty kilometres away but a thousand metres higher, a bureaucratic drawing-board vision made concrete. Ring binders stood on the slope in rank and file; three-storied duplexes with a view of the valley.

The inhabitants of New Tehri would be able to enjoy a vista of the flooded Old Tehri. But New Tehri does not function well. The bus station could have won a prize for its architecture, but it was orphaned—not a single boy selling spicy channa in newspaper cones. The pumps that were supposed to bring the water up from the valley broke down regularly; there were too few buses, so the transport costs sent the prices of all goods sky-rocketing. People still shuttled between Old and New Tehri, many had even moved back into the valley, determined to abscond from the future of this satellite township for as long as possible.

~

Deepak continued to rhyme and coin. Sometimes he moulded alliterations: ALERTNESS AVOIDS ACCIDENTS; sometimes he played around with nursery rhymes: THE ROAD IS HILLY, DON'T DRIVE SILLY. He was into rap: NO RACE NO RALLY, ENJOY THE BEAUTY OF VALLEY; he offered profound advice: THE SWEETNESS OF LIFE IS DEVOTION. Chinese influences could be discerned: LICENSE TO DRIVE. NOT TO FLY. He even seemed to be inspired by Kabir: DIFFICULT WILL BE DONE IMMEDIATELY, IMPOSSIBLE WILL TAKE SOME TIME. And once, just before the vista over the first major confluence of the Ganges, he succeeded in formulating the relaxed wisdom of a late worker: WHAT'S THE HURRY? RELAX, ENJOY AND PROCEED.

~

The Ganges is called the Bhagirathi until it meets the Alaknanda at Devprayag. Only after this confluence

32

is the river officially called the Ganges. A suspended bridge leads to a small town clambering up a steep incline. The *ghat* at the confluence is supposed to form the outline of India, according to the travel guide, but temporary flooding had washed away some of the coastal provinces. Behind the steps there are a few simple caves where pilgrims can stay overnight, even equipped with alcoves for the idols travelling with them. A *sadhu* squatted beside me as I took off my shoes. He showed me the blisters on his soles and asked for some money. Only then did he introduce himself.

Ashok Swaroop came from an ashram in Jaipur and was currently on the most celebrated of all the Himalayan pilgrimages, the Chardham *yatra*, a two-month journey to the four sacred sources— Badrinath, Kedarnath, Yamunotri and Gangotri. I asked him how he planned to complete the journey with his feet in such bad shape; he brushed aside my question and offered me his loaded *chillum*. I might have shared a few puffs with him, had I not been press-ganged into a *puja* by the high priest.

We stepped into ice-cold water. He chanted a few mantras that I repeated with little understanding and awful pronunciation. God was summoned to grant me, my wife, my parents and my grandparents a long and happy life. His delivery was rapid-fire, his tone mechanical, like water bursting from an opened sluice. Two teenagers observed us with suppressed mirth.

'How many prayers should we say for you?' asked the *pujari*. 'Hundred, five hundred, thousand?'

'Hundred,' I said, not interested in a bulk discount.

'And for your wife?'

'We'll share the hundred. Eighty for her, twenty for me.'

'No, no. Won't do. Minimum hundred per person. Nothing less.'

I agreed. It was the least I could do.

Later I sat down with a group of sadhus. One of them told me that his father had travelled for five years through Europe after the Second World War. He expressed his admiration for Hitler—not because of the Jews, not because of the war against the British

Empire, but because of the discipline! The man admired the *RSS*, the paramilitary organization that perceives the diversity and freedom of the Hindu tradition as a weakness and has launched a war of discipline against it—sometimes with the methods of the Scouts, sometimes with those of the Brownshirts. Another *sadhu* expressed his disgust of the British.

'Because of colonialism?' I asked.

'Because they eat meat and fish!'

Ever more pilgrims joined us. However, no respectful greeting, neither *Hari Om* nor *Gangaya Namaha*, could deter them from introducing themselves with a request for a donation. Finally I fled from this increasing degradation.

~

I thought I had understood Deepak's artistic motivation, but the metaphysics of his work, the vessel into which he poured his drops of poetry and warning, were revealed to me shortly before we reached *Rishikesh*: THERE IS NO SHORTCUT TO SAFE DRIVING. That is the key. There is no shortcut to salvation. One has to walk down, or more appropriately drive

35

down, the whole long and winding road, acknowledg-
ing the multitude of forms and names. As his complete
work became visible, I realized that Deepak had been
inspired by the Ganges *stotra*, the enumeration of 108
names of the goddess. He had formulated a respectful
paraphrase—108 mantras of traffic safety! A modern
adaption of an ancient form.

The sage's wet hair

We had barely reached *Rishikesh* when the monsoon
unleashed its pent-up violence. We could not drive
on because the wipers could not keep pace with the
downpour; the world outside could only be sensed.
We could not even get out of the car—the water
held the doors fast. Within minutes, the whole town
was submerged, transformed into an upland delta
with burns, ponds, waterfalls and flooded plains.
Patience huddled under all the eaves and every roof.
Those who were in a hurry had to roll up their
trousers, hold their shoes in their hands and venture
on to the flooded road—step by step through the
unknown. In the middle of the road in front of us, a

motorcycle had come to a halt, the exhaust spewing smoke; the two riders sat dazed, their feet ankle-deep in water, while the smoke grew denser and they continued to block the road. A woman in a simple sari crawled across the asphalt, half-swallowed by water, looking for something, coins perhaps, that she or someone else had lost. We were relieved to find a hotel at all on a day like this.

The most important instrument of contemporary spirituality is the loudspeaker; its volume set high as if the world were deaf. The *ghat* was dominated by an amplifier turned up to the pitch of ecstasy. Eardrums were stretched to the point of rupture. As we were about to leave, we were suddenly admitted to the heavenly abode of a power cut. At the Triveni *Ghat*, naked feet tapped on stones, a broom scraped across the ground, and on the bank murmuring voices circled around water, fire and existence. It was so quiet that I thought I heard the water soaking the saris of the bathing women. A man of noble bearing set down his green shopping basket on the last dry step. His white clothes were crisply pressed. He took out flowers, incense sticks and a *lota*. He performed his prayers with measured, exact gestures. Only the lips moved in his face. At the end of his *puja*, he took out a neatly folded newspaper, put his utensils into the basket and covered them with the paper—he seemed to have found solace in the ritual.

He strode away, ramrod straight and calm, and didn't flinch when the loudspeakers started blaring again. Joy and sorrow seemed to be one to him. The man disappeared behind a monumental sculpture, put up in 1990 and labelled with a PIN code (No. 753001). It represented the famous scene from the battle of Kurukshetra, the opening of the *Bhagavadgita*: the warrior *Arjuna*, hesitant to join the battle, and the charioteer Krishna; God with a human purpose, as beautiful as Guy Hamilton, who shows the way with an outstretched hand, an apocryphal bird perched on his index finger. Four foaming horses are pulling the battle chariot, *Arjuna*'s face is wrought with anxiety, his breastplate bears a crouching lion about to leap.

Everything is straining to attack; it is apparent that *Arjuna*'s qualms will not prevail.

As I left, the bird peeled off Krishna's finger and flew away.

～

Strict customs and stipulations about bodily purification are as old as civilization in India. The gods perceived bathing as a source of well-being; the myths are drenched with the cleansing power of water. Even five thousand years ago, in Mohenjo-Daro, the houses of wealthy persons were equipped with bathrooms and toilets; a drainage system led the water from the wells and directed the waste water into the canal system.

In each and every hotel in the country—irrespective of how unkempt or shoddy it may be—the guest can be sure of at least a pail of clean water. In our hotel in *Rishikesh*, the manager seemed to be a step ahead in the spirit of this tradition. A folded sheet of paper requested customers to share his concern for this most valuable environmental resource. He gave a list of possible savings:

Brushing your teeth	Close the tap	save 5–10 litres
Washing the face	Use a towel	save 8–15 litres
Shaving	Fill up the mug	save 8–15 litres
Shower	Turn off shower while soaping	(water-saving data not given)
Leakage	Please inform	save 400–3000 litres immediately

Leakage? If there had been only one leak! I notified reception immediately. A plumber appeared; he tightened and hammered away, but finally threw down his tools before the leakage. He defended his workman's pride, blaming the bad piping as water continued to leak from every tap.

~

In the Parmarth Niketan Ashram on the other bank of the river, we met Narendra, an old acquaintance, by sheer coincidence. He was a native of *Rishikesh* who had gone to Mumbai to work for Hindustan Lever, to support his family after the death of his father. One day, he realized that that he was only working but not living. He had not been able to save anything, because life in Mumbai was so expensive. He returned to *Rishikesh*. On the advice of his mother, he met Muniji, the high priest of the ashram, who talked briefly with him, before offering him a place in the ashram. Narendra used the word *sewa*—service—to describe what he was doing. Sewa, Muniji had said, is to attend to what is closest to one's heart, to do good deeds, to fulfil one's *dharma*. Narendra was happy, he was living again.

We stopped in front of the *gurukul*. Around eighty children, all orphans, were uniformly dressed in yellow robes. They were being imparted the traditional twelve-year training of the brahmachari, initiation into *Sanskrit* and the classical rituals. They were trained according to the old ideals of education—contemplation, the overcoming of desires, adherence to daily ritual, humility and obedience to the *guru*. Parampara, the teaching tradition, is inseparably linked to a *guru* who passes on the knowledge gained from his own *guru* to his disciples. We peeped through the window into a few bare classrooms. The children were sitting on mats along the wall, reciting verses in one voice. They were learning a Vedic hymn by rote, performing a series of exactly prescribed hand movements to match their sing-song recitation—a unique synchronized choreography. The path to error-free memorization leads through a valley of repetition. The more complicated the ritual, the more important it is to execute it perfectly. The slightest error threatens to disturb the cosmic order.

In ancient times, the students of a *gurukul* were divided into two groups: one where the students were trained in theology and the other where the students only learnt by rote (the vedapatis); each sloka was set, to the last detail, in a precisely defined tone and rhythm that did not vary across the country. Although the written work goes back a long way in India, about 1,500 years, orality has always had the upper hand in everyday life. The knitting of word and meaning to tone and rhythm guaranteed the accurate internalization of mantras and slokas. To safeguard him from distraction, the vedapati was never initiated into the meaning of the *Sanskrit* texts.

Salvation, while conserving energy

At Hari-Ki-Pairi, the footprint of Vishnu in *Haridwar*, we were intercepted by the uniformed activists of the Seva Samiti. They informed us sternly that donation was our duty for the upkeep of the ghats. A man of small stature and low rank hustled us towards a table behind which the tax collector was seated. With the first sentence I spoke in Hindi, the jurisdiction shifted from the corporal to the officer. Instead of a token donation, a substantial one was now on the cards. The officer opened a notebook and underlined with his nail several documented donations amounting to Rs 5,000, 2,000 and 1,000.

'We are keeping the *ghat* clean.'

'Very good!'

'We are looking after the safety of the pilgrims.'

'Very good!'

'We are looking after this precinct.'

'Very good!'

'We maintain law and order.'

I entered an amount of Rs 100 in the book.

'So little, sir? Hundred rupees, that's nothing for you—give us thousand rupees!'

'Hundred rupees is not much,' I agreed, 'but if I donate thousand rupees at every *ghat* along the Ganges, in Garhmukteswar, in Bithur, in Kanpur, in Allahabad, in Mirzapur, in Varanasi, in Patna, in Monghyr, in Sultanganj and Sahibganj, in Behrampur, in Calcutta and in Ganga Sagar, I'd become a pauper.'

'At the other places,' the man retorted, 'you can donate less—but in *Haridwar* demonstrate your generosity!'

I handed him a hundred-rupee note and laid a one rupee coin on it.

'Wah! This foreigner knows how to donate correctly. Wah! Do you also know why you have to give that extra rupee?'

'Well,' I answered, 'the hundred rupees are for the humans and the one rupee is for god.'

The activists had a hearty laugh; actually the zero is an inauspicious number because it implies the void. The pittance of a donation was excused.

The proceedings at the Hari-Ki-Pairi were a mixture of picnic, fair and ceremony. Local children used the *ghat* as a swimming pool; they jumped from the pedestrian bridges into the water and let the current zip them to the next bridge, where they clambered up the iron chains that hung like lianas, expressly placed there for this purpose. As daylight waned, the *ghat* filled up; the uninitiated were asked to sit down. Activists of the Seva Samiti stood by the bank within earshot of each other and with hoarse voices made every effort at converting good pilgrims into better donors. A gong was struck, voices tuned up, the activists ducked and vanished like masters of ceremonies who are surprised to find that the curtain has risen.

'Victory to Mother *Ganga*. Victory to Mother *Ganga*.'

Again we were at the mercy of the loudspeakers.

'Whoever thinks of You will have all his desires fulfilled.'

Ever more voices accompanied the loudspeakers, the twilight was lit up by ever more lanterns.

'Whoever finds solace in you shall overcome the sea of existence.'

Oil wicks were lit, the lamps were moved in circles.

'Thanks to your grace there will be light in all the three worlds.'

Directly above the *ghat*, next to a pedestrian bridge, a neon signboard sponsored by Indian Oil was aglow with suggestions that scrolled across it in large red capitals: 'Lower tyre pressure consumes 10% more petrol. Correct switching of gears saves 20% petrol. Whoever sings the *aarti* daily—switch off engine at a signal and save 20% petrol—shall achieve *moksha* effortlessly.'

Pilgrims sent leaf-boats laden with offerings of flowers and burning camphor on a journey. As the boats began to sink, the congregation slowly dispersed.

It rained again the next day, and the mythological sculptures in front of the government guest house in *Haridwar*, on an island between two canals, shivered slightly, like actors in a tableau vivant. When the sun focussed near and far, the lawn glistened, and the sculptures gazed at the sluice to their right.

The chief water engineer, Mr Sinha, welcomed me to his spacious office on the ground floor of the guest house. We sank deep into old armchairs. He told me that he could give me fifteen minutes of his time and immediately began drawing on a white sheet of paper, speaking and drawing and speaking for the whole of the fifteen minutes.

The first canal that branched off from *Haridwar*, he explained, was built by the British in 1843. Because of the strong protests by the Brahmins, who feared that the Ganges jal would be polluted by the steel of the sluices, the British could not build a dam. Thus the water remained pure, the canal empty, whenever the water level dropped. The Upper Ganges Canal was a grand structure, 1,500 kilometres long, the world's most extensive engineering feat at the time. At two points, intersecting rivers had to be led through aqueducts over the canal. The canal was the object of many study trips, artists enthused over the motif and specialists were amazed. It irrigated the Doab, the previously arid region between the Ganges and Yamuna.

'In 1987 we built a proper sluiced wall, as well as a third canal, through which we regulate the volume of water. Here we sit next to the first sluice on the main canal, through which we can determine how much water is siphoned off. Our colleagues from the agriculture department who are posted along the canal keep us informed, on a daily basis, about the volume of water required. We then let a maximum of 11,000 cusecs of water through. It would be easier to regulate if the water at the Hari-Ki-Pairi didn't need to be four to five feet deep because of the many pilgrims and VIPs who visit every day. Thus we have first to divert 30,000 to 40,000 cusecs of water from the river and then redirect at least two-thirds of it to the river after the *ghat*, because we follow the principle of never diverting more water from the Ganges than is absolutely necessary. We therefore have several so-called overflow canals between the *ghat* and the sluice, through which the water can flow back to the river. In my opinion we thus not only fulfil the requirements of agriculture but also adequately account for the ecological balance of the river.'

After the engineer had sketched out everything, down to the most minute detail, I put out my hand to accept the sheet of paper with thanks; but he folded it and tucked it away nonchalantly in his shirt pocket. When I asked him if he could please leave the sheet behind for my reference, he answered that that would be possible only if I could present the requisite letter of permission from the ministry in Delhi, after which he politely took his leave.

～

In the Mansa Devi *mandir* on the southernmost hill of the Shivalik mountains, a grizzled *sadhu*, evidently kept alive only by his prayers, stands in front of a young, decked-out priest wearing a heavy gold watch and gold-plated jewellery around the neck and arms. The young priest hands a ten-rupee note from the overflowing donation pot to the old man. The old man is confused. The young man tries to thrust the note into the old man's hand, the old man refuses it with growing resoluteness, as if he wanted to say, I am too old to start making such compromises.

～

Haridwar is a holy city where alcohol, meat, fish and even eggs are forbidden. To commit sin, one has to take the southward road to Sodom and Gomorrah. When we asked the rickshaw-wallah to take us to Jawalapur he turned around and whispered like a conspirator, 'Chicken, *haan?*'

Actually we were in the mood for a beer; it was my birthday. On the broad exit road there was one vegetarian restaurant after another. First the restaurants vanished, then the bright-lit shops, then the multi-storeyed solid houses. We had crossed the invisible boundary between *Haridwar* and Jawalapur. The street was no longer lit. Trucks hulked on either side of the street. Not a trace of drivers or goods. A few strays surfaced from the dark and yelped at our rickshaw. The rickshaw-wallah dodged them and dead-panned, 'Jawalapur.'

We were having second thoughts. At the next crossing, lit by a solitary lantern, the driver turned around again and asked after our wishes.

'Chicken?'

'No, beer, alcohol.'

'Chicken?'

'No!'

A few hundred metres later he pointed to a street-side stall. A few crippled tandoori broilers—marinated in orange—were impaled on skewers.

'Chicken!' shouted the rickshaw-puller with full-bodied hope.

'No,' we said, 'we want to sit down somewhere.'

He stopped again in front of a restaurant, a lone plastic table in the open, at which four men were attacking a mountain of tender legs. Their fingers were coated with orange juice, and fat flowed over their forearms. The only person without a chicken leg in his mouth told us how to get to a restaurant that served beer.

'Chicken, chicken, chicken,' the driver mumbled as he turned. We crossed a district of dereliction, coughed up a hillock and parked in front of a motel-like building, next to an armada of motorcycles and cars. It was dimmer inside than outside. Gradually we realized that the restaurant was full. Some of the niches were occupied by men on their boys' night out, others by large families. We were welcomed into the plot.

'Do you have alcohol?'

The waiter lowered his head as if he wanted to share a secret with us and mumbled, 'Chicken tikka, chicken makhani, butter chicken . . .'

'Beer?'

'No, we do not have, but mutton biryani maybe?'

'No.'

'Sheekh kebab maybe?'

'No!'

'Beer? That is six kilometres away.'

It was time to give up.

On our way back to *Haridwar*, we asked to be dropped in front of a vegetarian fast-food restaurant. At the next table sat a man whose fine intellect was calligraphed on his face. He smiled at us, we began to talk about Indian literature before the dosas, which were the size of papyrus rolls, were served. When the man heard of our search for hidden vice, he announced that he could at any time show us where to find beer, whisky and any other sins.

We dedicated ourselves to the *dosa* rolls, concentrating hard on making sure that the filling, small pieces of spicy potato, didn't fall out. When we had cleaned our fingers in lemon-water bowls, the man drew his chair closer to our table and proclaimed that, since we were so interested in India, he would have to tell us of another and very different sin.

He mentioned the name of the largest local para-statal (BHEL), one of the few profitable public sector undertakings in India and one of the world's largest manufacturers of generators and transformers as well as ordnance, a gigantic corporation, with 69,000 employees, 12,000 of them being engineers. At first sight, an exemplary undertaking. The employees live in their own colonies, which are equipped with excellent schools and hospitals. They are socially cared for and enjoy job security.

'I thought I should try and win BHEL as a customer for the foreign company I was representing. During my first visit, I was given a polite and friendly welcome; they heard me out, but were non-committal. I sent documents, attractive offers and many emails, but we received no orders. After my second visit, one of the employees, a nondescript subordinate, took me aside after a series of official appointments and said, "If you want to sell something, sir, you must give my boss money and I will tell you how this works. Drive to Jawalapur, to the cycle shop on the main road, everybody knows the shop, and present yourself before this gentleman." He wrote a name on a piece of paper. I did, in fact, find this man in the cycle shop. He was neither an engineer nor did he have any knowledge of the subject, but he assured me with great self-confidence, "Of course, I can put you in touch with the key people." He proved to be a free-lance agent for several foreign ancillary suppliers, an agent who was as small and at the same time as important as a pivot. He got me in touch with the concerned persons in the purchase department and other departmental heads, our business started to move and ever since, he gets a 5 per cent commission on each deal. He collects the payments for the AGDL managers. We openly transfer money to his Indian bank account; any authority can trace it. The payments to this agent appear in our balance sheet. I sometimes get calls from one of the persons in the purchase department who threatens to block the order if he doesn't receive further payment. You must understand that AGDL needs our copper coils in order to remain competitive at the international level. However, our deliveries are sometimes blocked by the doctored test reports of an engineer. We need to grease the palms of this employee if we do not want to lose our consignment. The gentlemen sometimes ask for golf clubs, sometimes some pleasure trips or a weekend trip to Bombay for the entire family. And this system spans the entire gamut—from the secretary all the way to the top boss.'

We were less surprised than the man had expected us to be. India was very much like the rest of the world.

A relative of a friend, the ex-Chief Secretary of Uttar Pradesh, had implored us to get permission for a boat ride from *Haridwar* down the Ganges. When he described to me the long bureaucratic path that the application had to traverse, I had the feeling that I would experience the end of *Kali Yuga* before the official approval arrived.

'Also,' the erstwhile Chief Secretary emphasized, 'you definitely need protection. A few policemen must accompany you; after all, we are responsible for you. The area is very dangerous, infested with bandits, call them dacoits, thugs or *Naxalites*. Haven't you read today's *Hindustan Times*? Get yourself a copy. This is no joking matter!'

The issue in question proved to be a journalistic cabinet of horrors. There was a report from Kanpur that three dozen 'desperados' had attacked a train, gunned down two policemen and kidnapped several passengers after looting the higher class. As usual the article concluded that the police had no clue about the identity of the criminals. The Lucknow correspondent, on the other hand, reported that the marriage season between two *adivasi* groups, the Bawarias and the Sansis, had commenced, with unpleasant consequences for the other inhabitants of the region. The tradition of these 'killer tribes' obliged young men to slay someone as a sort of initiation. No murder, no wife, was the rule. Someone lacking the killer instinct would never become an eligible bachelor. Consoling the privileged readers of this newspaper, the writer added that the victims were rarely well off. To round it off, there was an agency report from Aligarh about a gangster who was shot by the police during an encounter in broad daylight in the bazaar.

A brutal jungle was growing rampant beyond the ordered urban domain, into which it was best not to venture; but if contact was unavoidable, one should at least be heavily armed with the guarantees of one's own power. The way he was trying to persuade me, my interlocutor seemed to think that he was rescuing me from a great misfortune. We preferred to shun such protection.

The depths of the swamp

Two boys with grazed shins, a cowherd with a piece of driftwood in his hand, a *sadhu* who was having a bath, a rickshaw-wallah who had never driven heavily-laden passengers across this bumpy dam observed me as I pumped up our inflatable dinghy. We had deposited this boat on arrival in an ashram in *Haridwar*. It was a Czech model of robust, tested material. The boys automatically handed us our luggage and I secured it. They waved as Pac and I pushed out into the water and were picked up by the current. While we were whirling around our own axis—we had only practised paddling together at a swimming pool in Mumbai, gawked at by workers on a neighbouring construction site—the Shivalik ranges were left behind. For a moment we could see the Triyugi peak, named after the Treta Yuga. The last hillock vanished behind the reeds. We were alone in the plains, distrustfully eyed by buffaloes standing in the water, herons circling above their heads.

The first people we came across, a few hours later, were a few men sitting on pumped-up tyres and chatting animatedly. When we reached them, they stared at us as if we were ghosts. We stopped paddling and chatted with them while drifting this way and that on the current. A two-hour journey on the river separated the men from their village. They would arrive after sunset. As no road led to their village and none of them possessed a boat, they had to—when they wanted to visit *Haridwar*—drift downriver until they reached the first bridge and the nearby railway station. They then travelled by train to *Haridwar* to finish their shopping, the folded inner-tubes under their arms. They walked back to the Ganges, blew up their tubes and sat down on the river, in a good mood of patience. 'But where is all your shopping?' we asked.

The men acted as if it was a big secret, one grinned from ear to ear, another rolled his eyes, unwrapped his turban and proudly showed us the packets on his head: flour for *roti*, sugar and tea for *chai*. Suddenly, one of the men called out and they began to paddle vigorously with their hands and feet. Our boat drifted towards a tributary and we had, with belated recognition, to paddle powerfully back into the middle of the stream. The men grinned and warned us against the moody whirlings of the Ganges. They could read the flow precisely, we were the illiterates.

We wondered at how uninhabited the Ganges was. In the vanishing daylight, we paddled past a half-destroyed village. The stream had demolished several huts. A few people were standing among the ruins, quiet and immobile, staring at us. They were dressed in rags. They did not acknowledge our greetings, except for a girl who raised her arm diffidently and immediately dropped it, as if this gesture had no meaning. An explosion: the ruins of a hut slipped with its loamy foundation into the water. The people jumped back, the waves almost capsized us. The villagers laughed and ran along the bank. We shared an experience that bridged the distance between us. They ran and waved until they could no longer keep pace with our fast-vanishing boat.

We soon reached the Balawali bridge, about thirty kilometres from *Haridwar*. Near a temple a group of people had gathered around a funeral pyre. The river was so wide that we could only occasionally see the other bank. Our side of the bank was steep and slushy, there was no way of camping on the turf. Harried by the onset of darkness, we finally found an even surface, barely larger than our tent and at the water's edge. We didn't even have place to try out the kerosene stove that we had acquired in the bazaar in *Haridwar*.

Next morning, as early as six o'clock, we welcomed our first guests. The men from the nearby village were polite and curious. They were on their way to collect firewood; their bodies, dressed in rags, had never received an extra meal. Their knowledge of the river spanned until the next bridge. The city of Kanpur meant nothing to them. Being worried about the boat, we politely refused to accompany them to their village and started off through mild mist and a drizzle. Sky and water were flowing together, the dark shores hatched danger. The surface of the water was an opaque crust that no flying fish had pierced. As the rain petered out, the river was newly woven in shades and patterns that could only be discerned at close quarters.

There was drumming behind us. We turned around to find a shower coming towards us, the drops striking the water like hooves, galloping over us and leaving us drenched. When the sun asserted itself at noon, we could not see the shore for the thick reeds; our map translated this loss of bearings into shaded zones that had appeared in place of the clear blue line. We were often buffeted by sandbanks right in the middle of the river. It was not always easy to locate the depths. Whenever the river branched, we let the current decide our direction. This later proved to be a big mistake. When we realized that we had entered a tributary, the strong counter-current did not allow us to turn back. I assumed that the water would join the main river somewhere; instead, we landed in a swampy delta, the water course narrowed down, and the current ebbed until finally it vanished. Even if I stood in the boat, I could see nothing but the white flowers of the *kusha* grass. We drifted about in the delta until it struck us that we risked never finding our way out. We decided to follow the sun, consistently in the direction in which we supposed the main river to lie. Should we err, we would at least have reached the western shore. The direct route led through thick reed. The boat was enmeshed in grass and creepers. We poled, we seized the reeds in front of us and pulled ourselves forward. Pac drew at the paddle and started cutting a path through the grasses. When it was impossible to go further, I stepped out of the boat and immediately sank chest-deep into the mire. On my own, I could hardly have got out. We had no idea of the distance we had covered. The whole world seemed overgrown by rushes. Ganges had withdrawn herself from the human dominion and dragged us away as hostages.

The boat was covered with pollen, thorns and vines; we were completely drenched and our energy was depleted. We had just resigned ourselves to spending the night on the boat when the reeds gave way to a small pond. On one side, the ground was solid enough for us to drag the boat to a slightly drier area and to explore the surroundings on foot. We maintained contact with each other through regular shouts. One of Pac's shouts was alarmingly different from the previous one. I ran through the rushes, scratched on the arms, legs and face by the all-pervading sharp tips. When I found Pac, only her head, neck and arms were visible, as if she were in the middle of some mud-bath treatment. I pulled her out, we swore and laughed, and poled on, amphibian creatures, unsure where our skin ended and the swamp began. Later we came across a canal that was deep enough; the water almost reached my waist. We decided to drag the boat against the current until we came to the main river. I waded through the water, pulling the boat on a rope behind me, distant relatives of the tsetse fly feasting on my neck. It took hours, but slowly the tributary widened and the reeds began to thin out. We began to imagine the vista of the main river in the fullness of its beauty. The fainter and weaker I grew, the more vividly I painted our salvation. My body was thoroughly soaked, my hands seemed covered with turtle-skin. The light was just enough to see a sliver of horizon and the horizon was for us Land Ahoy! Finally the canal bent, I heaved myself on to the boat and marvelled with what lightness we flew on a broad stream full of promise. We soon found a beautiful camping place on a sandbank, closed our eyes in a moment of gratitude, and frolicked in the water to celebrate reconciliation with the multi-armed *Ganga*.

In the early morning the curtain of mist had not lifted, as if we were to be hidden from the world. In the past such misty curtains were conjured up by a *rishi* who wished to seduce a fisherwoman. No wonder many children had been found in the mythical swamp. So, too, the long-awaited son of *Shiva* bearing the name Saravanodbhava—the one born in the swamp.

A knock on *Shiva*'s door, a knock announcing the restlessness of the mortal gods and humans, a festering impatience that leads to thoughtless, foolhardy actions. *Shiva* and *Parvati* are united. It is easy to say this, but who can imagine the copulation of gods? The duration, the depth of feeling, the concentration, the heat. All classical texts of love and longing—the *Ananga Ranga*, the *Kama Sutra*, the *Koka Shastra*— have tried to glorify physical love, but they have only been able to climb a few rungs of a ladder that disappears in the clouds. At all times, sex remained something earthy—the sweat, the semen, the slime—and the conception of the united pair on Mount *Kailash* very vague.

When *Shiva* opens the door—the breakers of the peace did not give up, even though he kept them waiting outside for several years—his erection juts out as a truly natural *lingam*. The mortal gods are embarrassed but they cannot afford embarrassment. They avert their eyes, but their feet shuffle forward. In this moment of distraction, *Shiva*'s self-control gives way and, to his astonishment, he sees his semen shooting out. Agni reacts faster than thought; he throws himself forward, mouth open, and saves the semen from being wasted. *Shiva* is bemused, but *Parvati*, who appears suddenly behind him in a night-robe, crushed by anger, spews curses most unbecoming of the mother of the universe. The gods slink away, with Agni, at the end of the line, eaten up by pain, his gums, his tongue corroded.

As soon as they descend to the plains, Agni spits the semen into the Ganges where she broadens out, where she swells like a womb, where she grows marshy and gets matted in the *kusha* grass. The semen glows in the water like tiny shining fish. The Krittikas, the seven stars in Taurus, virgins who hanker after the dreams of sheltered princesses, are hypnotized by the glow. They leave heaven—six of them, to be precise; one, the eternal voice of dissent, does not move from the constellation—and slide into the water. The semen penetrates into them through the pores; they become heavy; together they carry the life blossoming within them. The mud and the marsh take care of them, until they open their fair bodies and bring forth a son: Saravanodbhava, also called *Skanda*. It is very lonely in this stretch of the Ganges, but innumerable pairs of eyes witness this event: all informers of the world, sent out by the impatient gods. Soon they will announce in the palaces and hermitages that the world has been saved because to *Shiva* a son is born. (The narrative mastery of the early myth-shapers: the downfall of *Taraka* is noted in passing. Since the world had found its balance again, with the birth of *Shiva*'s son, they deemed it unnecessary to spell out the logical and inevitable consequence, the defeat of the demon. We, on the other hand, saturated by Hollywood and its adepts, revel in sheer endless showdowns that always end in the predictable triumph of Good over Evil and, in doing so, neglect the classical question: How does Good come into existence, how is it established on earth?) When the world is in equilibrium, there can be no error in the arithmetic. Therefore *Skanda* opens the six mouths of his six heads to be fed for the first time; he will remain eternally young and virile. Far away on Mount Kailash, *Parvati* feels her breasts swelling up with milk. All equations must balance out.

~

We were imprisoned by the early mist on our sand-bank and sipped Nescafé with milk powder—the latter being scoffed at by the lowing of bulls grazing somewhere in their own loneliness. We were closer than one *gaukos*, the old Indian measure that defined the distance at which a bull could be heard. The value of a human life, too, was once measured in cows: one life equalled a hundred cows.

A few hours later we came to a monumental Victorian bridge—the Raoli barrage. We paddled to the eastern bank until we reached a moorage under a shady willow. On the embankment, bundles of grass were being loaded on to trucks. In the shade of the willow sat a representative of a Muzaffarnagar factory with thick wads of notes in one hand and a notebook on his lap, in which he entered simple equations: 300 kilos = Rs 51. He scribbled stingy invoices on pages that he tore from his notebook. The farmers stashed away the money in their dhotis; we had seen them before, towing their overloaded boats along the banks of the river, bent forward, grimacing, reminiscent of Russian serfs or the slaves of ancient Egypt. There was a peculiar asymmetry between the business-like casualness with which the well-fed, suited and booted representatives of industry doled out the money and the respectful gesture with which the villagers accepted the payment, brought the notes to their foreheads and hearts and then buried them in the few folds of their poverty. The distance to Muzaffarnagar was only sixteen kilometres, but the way there led through a regime of terror defined by rigid tradition and ignorance. In the weeks before our departure, this area had often appeared in print: short messages from the dusty *aangans* of hell. In Alinagar-ka-Majra, the village council, with the consent of both families, had sentenced a young couple to death by hanging for having committed the crime of falling in love although they belonged to different castes. Many children must accept the marriages arranged by their parents. A few weeks later, a seventeen-year old girl had swallowed poison in Sisonia after her family had locked her up because of 'unacceptable love' and had tortured her; her lover presumed that they may have killed her. In half a year, forty-seven young women had run away from home; their parents suspected they had been kidnapped. But in most of the cases, the explanation was a love affair that transcended caste and in a few cases even the divide between Hindu and Muslim. Running away from home was the only option.

An ice-cream vendor appeared on the embankment with his bicycle. The men invited us to an ice-cream. They treated us with courtesy, they offered their help. They fell silent when two policemen appeared who confined their attention to our inflatable dinghy. The mood was friendly, relaxed. It was difficult to imagine that these men came from villages where young lovers were lynched. Until one considered that they stalked through marshland every day, cut reeds, broke their backs and traded their dignity for Rs 17 per bundle. Each encounter with the world of the torn-out receipt threw their sense of worthlessness back at them. They clung to the safety rope of inherited order, the only surplus value to their existence.

They told me of the Vidur Kuti temple, some way down the river—surely I knew it from the *Mahabharata* (Vidur was the wisest of men, kuti the simplest of huts). When they felt that it was time for us to leave, they rose and carried our boat across the barrage to where we could launch it again. Only one of them asked for money and was immediately rebuked by the others; we took noisy leave of one another.

Soon the temple came into sight, but there was a huge, overgrown sandbank before it, and we were at a loss to know how to negotiate a way round it. An old fisherman—skin and bones, with a net full of holes—tried to explain to us how to get there, in an incomprehensible dialect. He then asked us for food. We showed him our rationed stock of soup sachets and Maggi noodles and were sad to have to refuse him. He turned away without a word, as if he hadn't expected anything else. Even the wise Vidur could offer Krishna only wild green spinach.

～

Alexander the Great was convinced that the Ganges formed the outermost boundary of the earth. He probably placed his trust in the first map that showed India, the map by Mecataeus. Neither he nor his army ever reached the Ganges, but his conquest inscribed India into the European idea of the world. Until the end of classical antiquity, the Ganges flowed somewhere between legend and speculation. Virgil compared the floods of the Ganges with an army going to war (*Aeneid*); Ovid sang the praise of Bacchus's journey to the 'wide flowing Ganges' (*Tristia*). The church fathers, St. Eusebius being the first among them, supposed that this river, flowing at an eschatological distance, was the Phison, the first river of paradise. Throughout the Middle Ages, the Ganges denoted the end of the world. Paradise has been drawn, in an anonymous map from seventh-century AD

Ravenna, as a small round island facing the mouth of the Ganges (perhaps a Sri Lanka that's slid away slightly?). Eden remained in India through the Middle Ages. A popular legend tells of the adventurous journey of Eirek the Norwegian in search of *Paradisus extra Gangem*. Dante, in his *Commedia*, mentions the Ganges twice; in Christopher Marlowe's drama, Doctor Faust is standing on a peak in the Caucasian mountains and looks down into paradise, where the Ganges (alias Phison), the Nile, the Euphrates and the Tigris are flowing. The cartography of the modern era stripped the Ganges of such myths after Christopher Columbus, who believed himself to be in India, wrote to his king on 7 July 1503 that the natives had assured him that 'from the (nearby) province of Ciguare, it would only be a ten-day journey to the river Ganges'.

~

Sometimes the Ganges flowed silently, light eddies wetting her mute mouth. There was little to see, little to hear. I stretched out my feet, heels brushing the water, and entrusted the boat to the current. We saw birds, storks and herons, who let themselves be carried along the river on twigs, the lines of their feet crossing in reflection, and, around ten kilometres south of Raoli, a dolphin. The grey-brown animal leapt over the water in an elegant ellipse. We were swimming naked in the river, with one hand on the boat; we craned our necks, disbelieving, to catch a second glimpse of the mammal. It seemed plump, well-rounded. In the villages along the river, the children grew up with a legend that the dolphins, called *susas* on account of the noise they make when they surface to catch a breath, were land mammals who had jumped into the Ganges when she was born. Other legends were similar to mermaid stories, like the one about the princess who took a daily bath in the Ganges, which she reached by a secret path leading directly from the palace to the riverbank. One day, seeing the king, her father-in-law, approach, she begged *Ganga* to hide her, so that he would not see her naked, at which *Ganga* transformed her into a dolphin.

Soon afterwards, in a village next to the bank, in which a water pump was buzzing, we found a seat on a *charpoy* in front of a few reed houses with walls askew. A young farmer brought us fresh well water.

'Yes,' he said, 'we do see the susas pretty often. We like them, they bring us good fortune.'

I asked if the village had ever been threatened by the river. 'Our village used to be there,' the farmer pointed into the river. 'We have had to shift twice. *Ganga* wanders. In a few years, I think, we will have to shift again. *Ganga* is coming closer and closer.'

The river's restlessness along its upper course hinders long-term human settlement. *Ganga* drives her followers before her. The village consisted of forty inhabitants, rice, corn and vegetable fields, a few bullock-carts and a small jetty two kilometres downstream. The man offered us lunch; we excused ourselves. The entire village accompanied us back to the boat.

In the evening, camping on a sandbank in the middle of an estuary, we heard two sounds in the distance: the trumpeting of a bull and the tinny sound of a transistor. Then again, a large silence. We made tea in front of the tent and savoured it along with the sunset, sunk in a reverie of birds turning into silhouettes plunging into the fast-falling night, leaving nothing behind but a fluttering imprint. Then we prepared a portion of Maggi two-minute noodles and mixed it with a stock soup. For dessert there was a small piece of *halwa*, and a cigarette sounded the final note of the meal. Sometimes a piece of the opposite bank would break off and slide into the water. The noise disquieted us each time. It symbolized an uncertainty that was larger than the restlessness of the Ganges.

Tigri was the first major settlement we reached after six days on the boat—a village that boasted a tailor's place with a shop window. For the first time since *Haridwar*, we saw walled houses with courtyards and a few square metres of prosperity. Cattle rearing was apparently profitable. There were services worth mentioning, a bazaar, and even an English-medium school.

'Oh, then you know English!'

'No,' was the curt response. 'We are learning English but we are not speaking.'

The bazaar street ended in the vegetable market. Plastic awnings cast shadows on the ground, within which heaped tomatoes, cucumbers, potatoes and onions were sold by the pyramid. While buying tomatoes we learned that from Gajraula station there was a direct train to Lucknow; from there Kanpur, the largest city on the Ganges, was just a stone's throw away.

While paddling we could not get the convenient train connection out of our minds. Over the next few kilometres, flanked on both sides by marsh and *kusha* grass, we wondered whether it wouldn't be a better idea to break our journey at the small town of Garhmukteswar, where the Ganges had assumed human form, married King Shantanu and produced eight sons, seven of whom she drowned in the Ganges because they were celestial beings who were under a curse of rebirth. But by sparing the eighth one, Bhishma, a new story was set in motion— the *Mahabharata*.

Just before the bridge at Garhmukteswar, we bumped against the steps of the *ghat*. A boatman was fast to react and grasped the boat firmly. Within moments the entire *ghat* was crowded with so many people that we could not see the steps. The small town was about a kilometre away. While Pac made her way to the railway station to inquire about the train, the ferrymen who row pilgrims to the other side of the river interrogated me. They wanted to know all about our experiences on the Ganges; they found it unbelievable that someone, a foreigner at that, had paddled all the way from *Haridwar* to Garhmukteswar. I gave away our kerosene stove to the smartest of the ferrymen and was thanked with his help, until we left. Those who had experienced our arrival told the latecomers, in a multitude of voices, of our journey. The mass of people proliferated, crept up to the bridge on which some passers-by enjoyed a balcony seat, jostling side by side. I acquainted myself with the people standing around me, while emptying the boat. One man wished to touch everything I carried on to land. Another stood so close that I had to bump into him, at which he retreated a step and then slowly edged forward again. A third man offered us advice for our onward journey, relentlessly repeating his wisdom which was exhausted in a single sentence.

Pac returned with a Sikh in western clothing in tow; he had fallen in with her on the road.

'Where are you going?'

'To my boat.'

'Where is your boss?'

'I don't have a boss.'

'No, but where is your boss now?'

'Nowhere.'

'What are you doing then?'

'Going to my boat.'

'What is your boat?'

'We are travelling.'

'Where to?'

'We stop here.'

'But you are going to your boat.'

'To the *ghat*.'

'Ah, to the *ghat*. Can I join you?'

We distributed the rest of our provisions among a few sadhus who were watching us with veiled curiosity from the highest step of the *ghat*. We carried our backpacks up to the road. The flat landscape and the straight asphalt strip had little to offer. I regretted having left the Ganges behind. We waited at the roadside for the next shared minibus. A monkey tried to open our backpacks; we shooed it away and, as it hopped off, it overturned a hawker's tray, and the peanuts, scattering in all directions, drew a horde of monkeys. A minibus stopped, the ferrymen gave us a ceremonial send-off; we were still waving as we sped over the bridge; we caught one last glimpse of the Ganges before lurching forward on to the Grand Trunk Road, the asphalted myth that spans northern India from Punjab to Bengal. The traffic reminded me of a rapid. The cars, always bumper to bumper, overtook one another narrowly. The stench that rose from the drain beside the road owed its existence to the Gajraula Industrial Estate whose effluent finally reached the Ganges. Now that we realized that the pollution of the Ganges began here, there was far less reason to regret our decision to continue the journey by land. We turned off the Grand Trunk Road. At the first red signal, passengers and drivers started bombarding us with questions. When they heard about our boat journey, they all shook hands with us.

Hardly had we reached the counter and asked for two tickets to Lucknow when the clerk exclaimed, 'Oh, you are the two people who have come down *Ganga*, you were in my village this morning, in Tigri. I know all about you! Come in, come in.'

While we carried our luggage into his office, we heard him tell his two colleagues about our journey and our stopover in Tigri.

'My name is Kishan Yadav,' he greeted us, 'and you are my guests, okay.'

We reminded him about the tickets.

'No problem, you are my guests now. Two sleeper berths in the ten o'clock express, okay? We cannot issue the tickets now, we shall do it at nine o'clock.

Have you seen the tailor's shop in Tigri, at the start of the bazaar? That is our family shop.'

He closed his shirt at the collar, ran a hand over the buttons and smoothed his slicked-down hair. He wore a loose white shirt, cotton trousers and moccasins without socks. We asked him where we could have dinner.

'There is only one place for you, the best one in Gajraula, but it's not walking distance. You must take a rickshaw, okay. I will make sure you are not over-charged ("overcharged" being the only English word he used).'

In front of the railway building he summoned a coolie, impressed upon him the fact that we would be departing by the ten o'clock express, that he should help us carry the luggage then, that he should under no circumstances overcharge because 'these here are my friends, understood!'

The coolie nodded, grinned and vanished.

'Otherwise, he would charge you Rs 15 or even Rs 20, you know,' said Kishan, and ran on to a rick-shaw-wallah whom he also showered with his excited sing-song. When, five minutes later, they were still arguing, I offered Rs 20 for the return journey and we were immediately invited to board the rickshaw. Kishan shook his head and mumbled 'overcharge'. He ran a few steps alongside the rickshaw, repeated the name of the restaurant and told the driver to inform the hotel owner that we were Kishan's guests and that he should under no circumstances treat us like other foreigners.

We had just turned on to the main road when the rickshaw-wallah stopped and squatted by the roadside to relieve himself. We had to stop again at a railway crossing. The waiting cycles, rickshaws and bikes began shoving their way forward along the lane meant for oncoming traffic. The same thing happened on the other side of the railway crossing. When the barrier was cranked up, when the engines howled and the headlights flashed, two full lanes confronted one another, bumper to bumper, wheel to wheel. Battle was joined. The two armies clashed on the battlefield of the railway crossing. Cars and trucks were jammed. Only two- and three-wheelers could make space for themselves by elbowing pedestrians off the road. Push for shove, they made use of every centimetre. All was fair, except giving way. We collided with another rickshaw whose patriarchal freight favoured me with a stern glare, as though I were personally responsible for the traffic jam. Minutes passed. The howling truck engines were empty threats; the rickshaw-passengers covered their mouths and noses with handkerchiefs. We rolled over the tracks, moving faster now that the road sloped downward; soon the driver could pedal again. I looked back: only survivors escaped from the cloud of dust and fumes, there was not a single victor. A little later we overtook a young man in tight sporty shorts and an immaculate polo shirt, Wimbledon-white, a tennis bag over his shoulder, a can of tennis balls in his hand. He sauntered along the barely-lit, potholed street.

The restaurant proved to be a typical dhaba, those eateries that line every Indian highway. A few tables and benches had been set outside, so close to the Grand Trunk Road that the owner could save on lighting, thanks to the many trucks passing by. Inside, the food, mostly vegetarian curries, was sizzling in cauldrons. One could peek into every dish. The rickshaw-wallah sat down at the adjacent table and drank a glass of water. We ordered a meal for him. It was an uncomfortable surprise for him. Suddenly Kishan appeared. Did we order the food for the rickshaw-wallah? How could we do that? When I explained to him that a satiated driver would get us faster to the railway station, he settled down and attacked the food that we had ordered for him too.

'Not to worry,' he said between bites, 'I will take care of everything, you were in my village. If I had been there, you could have stayed overnight in my house; we will be travelling together to Moradabad; if you want *chai*, you can also get *chai*. Now listen, what is this supposed to be? Rs 162? You should not overcharge them just because they are foreigners!'

'Overcharge?' asked the perplexed waiter.

'Ask your boss to check the bill.'

The poor waiter marched off with the slip of paper to the man sitting at a small table at the entrance. He looked up, Kishan waved out to him.

The waiter was back at our table at once and presented me with the same bill. Kishan snatched it out of my fingers.

'Here, what is this, Rs 32, what is that supposed to be for? Four times dal. Four times dal, really? How can three people eat four plates of dal? The rickshaw-wallah . . . oh, yes, okay, although, it still seems too expensive.'

As soon as we left the Grand Trunk Road behind us, we plunged into stumbling darkness.

'In Bombay, sometimes you get a five-minute power cut; here we go for six, seven, eight hours without power,' explained Kishan. 'But Gajraula is developed, we have a hospital here, the new building out there, most modern technology, the doctor has returned from England, he was a famous doctor there but he has come back to his native place, he has studied there for ten years.'

Kishan read out the foreign titles as naturally as if he were reading street names. Soon after we encountered the tennis ghost again. He sauntered in the opposite direction with feather-light steps, as if he were returning from the floodlit grounds of the Olympia Park.

At the railway station, Kishan jumped nimbly from the rickshaw and strutted into the building that was oversized and full of dark recesses. His colleague who had taken over the night shift explained that he could offer us only one sleeper berth on the ten o'clock express. Kishan stood at the counter and needled on: 'Surely it should be possible to find a way, if the will is there . . .'

Sharif, his upright colleague, reprimanded him. He could not bend the rules just because we were Kishan's friends. Kishan, it seemed, was eager to disagree. The two argued loudly, while one passenger after the other placed a few coins at the counter and had their tickets thrown at them. Sharif offered us two tickets for the train at eleven thirty, and we gladly accepted. Kishan shoved his face close to the grill and expressed the suspicion that Sharif wanted to 'overcharge' us, and that really shook up the sleepy railway station. Sharif screamed that he was an honest person and that he would not allow others to lead him astray. When he paused for breath, Kishan ran him through with another accusation. Sharif turned to me, and I hastened to assure him that I trusted him completely. He spoke of rates and connections, I said 'Yes' and 'Of course'. He calculated the final fare three times on a small pocket calculator, for me; this proved to be difficult, for the numerals sometimes did not glow, so Sharif had to read out what was not displayed. He then took up paper and pencil and added the figures once again, as slowly as if he were giving me a beginner's course in arithmetic. I thanked him profusely for his readiness to help, his friendliness and his understanding, and clutched the tickets firmly, anxious lest I lose them to another of Kishan's outbursts. Finally we picked up our backpacks and moved to a bench on the platform.

Kishan slunk away, deflated, a victim of his own grandiloquent promises. But he soon reappeared, accompanied by an overweight acquaintance whom he presented as Mr Raja involved in 'politics'. Mr Raja spoke in a soft voice that seemed to cry for attention. 'Disturbance', he said, 'you want to register disturbance?' (It soon became clear that 'disturbance' was to him what 'overcharging' was to Kishan.) We said no.

'I know the DM of Bhuj', he replied.

I hadn't a clue what he was talking about. He pulled a notebook out of a pocket, snapped it open and read out an address, his voice swelling with pride: District Magistrate, Mr So-and-so, Bhuj, Kutch, Gujarat, and a few telephone numbers. He sat next to me and diligently showed me the address, without being able to decipher its secret message. He wrote his name and telephone number on the next page, tore it off and ceremoniously handed it over to me. In turn I gave him my visiting card, which indicated that I was a journalist. He gave a satisfied nod and drew out a mobile phone. Pressing a few buttons, he held the mobile to my ear—thank god, busy. But Mr Raja was not a man to give up.

'This is the STD code for Bhuj, isn't it?'

'Yes,' I confirmed blindly, 'that really looks like the STD code of Bhuj.'

He then tried the number again and again, until finally he introduced himself to someone at the other end in a submissive tone and excused himself for 'causing disturbance' but with him was a foreigner friend who wished to speak to the district magistrate. The mobile was held to my ear again.

'Hello,' I said.

'Hello, hello,' the other voice snapped.

'That is the DM,' Mr Raja whispered, and looked at me, full of expectation.

'I really don't know what to say,' I stammered.

'Wrong number,' said the voice of the administrative chief of the western Indian province that had recently been devastated by an earthquake.

'Yes,' I happily agreed, a wrong number indeed, and ended the conversation.

Mr Raja's face looked like a collapsed soufflé. Whatever he had hoped to achieve from this talk with the DM had not materialized. He toyed unhappily with his mobile and mumbled, 'You know I am only a poor man.'

Before he could disturb the income tax commissioner of Kanyakumari or the protocol chief in

Guwahati at dinner, I snatched the mobile and started to dial our number in Mumbai till I realized that there was a certain danger of his saving the number and calling us up in the middle of the night during his next interesting encounter. Instead, I dialled the number of a friend and boasted that I had just spoken to the DM of Bhuj on the telephone. The friend opined that the Ganges had done me no good and hung up. I returned the mobile. Mr *Raja* was shocked but also unfathomably impressed. He stood up and explained to the bystanders that he had called up Bhuj and that, thereafter, I had spoken to Mumbai. And he held up the mobile as proof. I soon became a celebrity on the platform, the foreigner who had phoned Mumbai.

The ten o'clock train came and went, Kishan remained. 'Kishan, where does the S-1 bogie stop?' we asked.

'Not to worry,' said Kishan, his voice a little softer, 'I shall be with you. I shall look after you, okay. You are my guests. You were in my village.'

Trains chugged in, shrouded human forms like valueless luggage on their roofs. Passengers were

91

sleeping on the platform on mats or sheets that they had spread out. Sharif came to inform us that our train was delayed by two hours. 'He has a bad conscience,' said Kishan, and launched into another volley of abuse; this time, he did not spare even Sharif's Muslim faith. The sheen of the charming bon vivant had worn off completely. Mr *Raja* paid us two more visits, to bid adieu with the formula: 'Okay dear, go to sleep. Sorry for disturbance.'

When our train rolled in, it became clear that Kishan did not have the faintest idea where our bogie was. Burdened with around eighty kilos of luggage, we staggered after him. Neither S-1 nor S-2 nor any other Ss were written on the doors. Nobody answered Kishan's loud questions. The train started to move, Pac jumped on, I ran alongside the train, the dinghy in my arms, which I managed to throw into a compartment with my last reserve of energy, before jumping on. Kishan also heaved himself up, gasped for breath, looked around and announced with great satisfaction, 'We are in the right compartment.'

Ganga's
Tanned Skin

There is no creation
and there is no destruction . . .

Bithur, one of the centres of the universe, has lapsed into oblivion. Between the dilapidated houses, with their thin brick walls, myths slumber. After the world had been destroyed and regenerated, *Brahma* chose this site for his home. He created *Shiva* from the sand of *Ganga*, he held a *yagna* for ninety-nine years. Then he moved on—nobody is as restless as the gods. It is said that Dhruva meditated in Bithur for five, eight or thirty-six thousand years before he was promoted to the North Star. Not many people outside the region are aware of these localizations— legends are dressed in native costume, the hearth becomes home to spiritual role models. In Bithur *Valmiki* founded an ashram and wrote the *Ramayana*. He was the author not only of the epic but also of his own literary character. Sometimes it is hard to distinguish between who acts and who comments. The prototypical author *Vyasa* cohabits, as a stinking hermit, with two queens and a maid—true to the metaphor of artistic creation—and thus begets a substantial number of his characters himself. Did the gods foresee that the author they had commissioned to reduce their marvellous deeds to a humanly digestible measure would act the role of destiny with his ink and his sperm?

Sitting with our guide on a sprightly boat, we skimmed past fifty-two ghats. On the opposite side of the Ganges there were only reeds and rushes. A few isolated people inhabited the ghats, a woman beating clothes, two boys splashing water, an old man drawing his tongue out of his mouth. A plastic Bata sole floated in the river. The *mandir* that is traditionally filled with water when there is dire need for rain had gathered patina, but was not damaged. The domes of some of the other mandirs had collapsed, mud had crept into them and swallowed the abdomens of the relief figures. Fifty-two ghats for fifty-two rajas: that had once been the simple symmetry. But the kings had discontinued their pilgrimage to Bithur after the British ravaged the ghats in answer to the Great Indian Uprising of 1857.

Today it seems necessary to demonstrate the holiness of the location. Near the ghats a *sadhu* sat behind a bucket of water, showing off a floating stone on which '*Ram*' was spelt in large saffron letters. The *sadhu* defused rational objections even before they had been voiced. He pressed the stone into my hand: it was hard, heavy and not a bit porous. He threw a '*Ram*-less' stone into the water and it sank immediately. He gave me a look of great expectancy, as if I ought to authenticate the wonder.

'Did you know,' the guide continued, 'that the two sons of *Rama* were born in Bithur?'

'Why not?' I thought. 'If *Valmiki* lived here, what should have hindered him from settling his figures in Bithur.'

But the guide had already galloped ahead. He narrated a story that was new to me. Luv, a single child, disappeared one day. *Valmiki* formed a replica of him from *kusha* grass and breathed life into the second son, Kush. Later on, of course, they found Luv.

In India, someone once said, every legend is apocryphal, and therefore, all apocrypha must be true. As scenes and plots change from place to place, from mouth to mouth, the moral and political direction of the myths also changes. Besides the classical, Brahmanical epic of *Valmiki*, there are many other versions of the *Ramayana*—one drama, one hundred authors. One of the alternative accounts introduces *Rama* as a Buddhist and *Sita* as his wife as well as his sister. In a *Jain* version, *Rama* proves to be a staunch believer in *ahimsa*, and *Ravana* is presented not as a villain but as an enlightened being, devoted to the search for truth and wisdom. In Telugu there exists a 'feminist' retelling in which *Sita* is not subjugated to *Rama* and *Shurpanakha* takes revenge on him. A *Dalit* version implies that the killing of King Bali was part of a larger plan to oppress the lower castes,

Rama's task being to defend the strict hierarchy of caste and gender. According to several south Indian versions, *Ravana* leads the Dravidian resistance against the Aryan conquest. Because of its flexibility, the *Ramayana* even travelled outside of India, all the way to Indonesia and Cambodia. In Thailand King *Rama* I commissioned a group of poets to compose a national version that would enhance the sacred legitimacy of the kingdom. The result, the *Ramakien*, was to become the central foundation myth of the country, inspiring a multitude of other texts and dramas. Later kings of Thailand wrapped themselves in a painted version that runs along the inner side of the palace wall in Bangkok.

The stone on which *Ram* is written will not sink, and the story of *Rama* is holy to all, because it can be told and retold to suit everybody's interests.

~

We travelled to nearby Kanpur on a dirt-track hemmed in by gardens, farms, weekend bungalows, cricket pitches and water-parks. These were the retreats of Kanpur's rich. Every Saturday a local *paan-wallah*—his profits palace-high—invites his neighbours, the leather producers and the leather exporters, to a party. The rarest trees grow in his garden. Unfortunately the road no longer leads along the shore of the Ganges. The river has migrated northwards, six kilometres in thirty years, and its bed, left ownerless behind, has been occupied by those who possess nothing. They have built their huts and barracks on sand. These wretched squats will be flooded once the new weir within Kanpur's city limits is completed, an ambitious project costing years and crores that will divert the Ganges back into its original course and theoretically guarantee the water supply, control flooding and reclaim land. Not really a problem, because in any case the squats are 'illegal'. Then the weekend palaces will once again offer vistas of the river.

One day Govind Makhanwala decided that he couldn't take it any more—he launched a cleanliness campaign. A tall, white-haired gentleman, Govind lived with an extended family of three married brothers in the affluent colony of Azad Nagar. Although Kanpur is blessed with municipal refuse collectors, the garbage heaps in front of his house had grown into pyramids. If he wished to go for a walk with his wife, Raksha, they had to drive to the zoo nearby, the car windows rolled up, for the stench on the way was unbearable.

'One weekend we met with all our neighbours and we set off with wheelbarrows and spades. Businessmen, graduates, people who had never done manual work before. In the beginning, enthusiasm ran high. We collected the rubbish in a dump, and then, after some money had been raised and some patience, we convinced the council to have it collected.

'The community refuse disposal, with all its trucks and relatively well-paid employees, had for some time been selling its services on the free market to the highest bidder. If a school was keen on cleanliness, it made a deal with the disposal people, who swept the schoolyard clean and left the garbage on the side of the road. Thus the collectors earned two or three times more, and the school could guarantee hygienic standards.

'When I withdrew from our campaign because of work pressure, it petered out. There was no one to motivate the people, and they need to be pulled out of their lethargy. Today only one street in our area is regularly cleaned by the residents, and the difference from all the other streets is enormous. But that's the way we are: we clean our room and sweep the dirt in front of the door. We clean our house and sweep the dirt into the yard. We clean our yard and sweep the dirt on to the street, where it remains, for there is a distinct border between the private, for which one is responsible, and the public, for which no one is responsible. We pollute the Ganges, because she falls under the responsibility of the gods, not us. This mentality splits our humanity in half. We hoot at a cripple shoving himself along on a small cart, and if he doesn't get out of the way, we force him off the road, but we are prepared to do everything for a relative or a close friend. We live in a rigid, self-congratulatory culture that constantly flatters itself with the great achievements of the past: three thousand years ago we invented the zero! So what? What have we achieved since then? What is the use of a grand old tradition if it leads to such a paralysed society?'

~

I had read about Rakesh Jaiswal on the Internet. He had caused a stir some years ago when he started salvaging rotting corpses from the Ganges, at a bend, where they were entangled in driftwood and other stranded objects. Corpses of poor people, whose relatives could not afford the cremation cost of around Rs 1,000. During one dry season alone, he had, together with a few fellow combatants, taken about fifty half-decomposed, half-eaten corpses out of the river. That earned him some respect and the inhabitants of Kanpur started taking Rakesh and his organization—Eco-friends—seriously.

'I have never seen the Ganges so beautiful,' he said, a polite man with a rounded face and a soft voice, as we rowed out from one of the ghats. 'So much water, and so green. During the long dry season the Ganges shrinks to a sewer. One can wade from one side to the other, there is no flow. The stench is horrible.'

We drifted down the river, past fishermen and buffaloes, past an ordnance factory and a golf course, past a few trees with fuzzy crowns.

'Seven or eight years ago, one day black muck gushed out of the taps at home. We had to wash with this water and, even worse, it was the only water we had to drink. Kanpur is the second largest industrial city along the Ganges, all the sewage is poured into the river; the factories draw all the water they need from her and they drain the poisonous waste water back into her.'

Shortly after passing the old Old Ganges Bridge, which dates back over a hundred years, Rakesh pointed out a narrow canal, secreting a greenish-blue, oily liquid, one of the many illegal drainages of the city's four hundred tanneries. A few men were fishing nearby, kids were playing in the water.

'A few years ago the Allahabad High Court declared three hundred factories closed: silk-weaving mills in Varanasi, carpet workshops in Mirzapur, quarries in *Haridwar*. The industries were ordered to pre-clean their waste water. Most of them conformed to this injunction and were allowed to resume production. Unfortunately the closures mostly affected small companies that found it difficult to carry out ecological investments.'

On the shore stood a few time-honoured bungalows from colonial times, when the wealthy sought the riverbank for their villas, but the successful industrialists and businessmen of today have withdrawn. Slums dominate the area, especially in the densely populated Jajmau quarter with its many tanneries.

'Water-related illnesses like hepatitis have reached epidemic proportions. In many areas the ground water is also contaminated. We have proven high levels of ammonia and chromium in our food. But until today there hasn't been a single scientific study of the correlation. We know that the inhabitants of the twenty villages further downstream, who use *Ganga* water for irrigation, suffer massively from skin diseases and asthma.'

We landed and drove to the city's most modern sewage plant in an autorickshaw that trailed a black plume of smoke behind it. Rakesh seemed well acquainted with the engineers. The man in charge put on a brilliant show of rhetorical disorientation, as if I was a foreign investor interested in buying the plant. He spoke of anaerobic techniques. He spoke of biogas generators that overcame the regular power failures. He spoke of clean water that was sold to farmers. Rakesh sat next to me and never said a mumbling word. After the presentation we drank some *chai* and conversed pleasantly.

'A complete success,' I pronounced. 'The Ganges will be clean soon.'

The engineers were discomfited at having convinced me so easily.

'We do have our fair share of problems,' they objected. 'We lack funds. Until last year we were financed by a Dutch project. We should have received payment for the clean water we deliver to the farmers, but the municipal corporation is completely inefficient. And the government of Uttar Pradesh refuses to support us, because, according to plan, we should be financially self-sufficient.'

Back in our rickshaw, I threw Rakesh a perplexed glance. He gave me a shrug.

'What's the use of a sewage plant that doesn't function? They do generate their own power, but the waste water first has to reach them through a series of pumping stations, and these stand idle every day.'

Yukti, the Makhanwalas' eldest daughter, works at a call centre for General Electric, where twelve hundred Indians sit cheek by jowl in a large open-plan office, staring into screens that advise and orient them in everything they do. She is on the telephone all working-day long. A customer calls from a suburb in Atlanta; he requests servicing for an appliance; she asks him whether he has a service contract or whether he will pay cash; she searches in the system for a technician in Atlanta with a free slot; she says a friendly goodbye: Thank you very much for calling and have a nice day.

The Indian voices must be informed about the weather in the USA (hurricane in Florida, Montana snowed in). Yukti was trained in an intensive course to understand the various US accents; TV serials, soap operas and radio shows served as her tutors. Her intonation had to be demusicalized. Sober pronunciation is called for. The Indian voices have to be up with the important social and political developments, should a question regarding a payment that has gone astray lead to some chewing of the fat. And if a customer inquires whether one is American, the voices should answer vaguely but under no circumstances reveal themselves as Indian. In some of the call centres, changing floors is like changing continents. On the ground floor, British accents attend to British customers, the first floor is American, and the second floor is worked by the Australian stand-ins.

Large billboards promise a future in call centres, MTV India raves about a dream career as a call centre operator. More than ten thousand Indians have found work—Uncle Sam wants you too! Govind Makhanwala, who as one of the initiators of 'The Resurgent Kanpur' actively pushes for a training centre, knowingly reports that in England, which for many educated Indians is still the measure of all things, more people answer phone calls than slave in the coal, steel and automobile industries. But he does not mention that every second employee resigns within a year, citing monotony, stress or night shifts. Govind nurtures the vision of a flowering Kanpur. But his is a lonely struggle. 'In India,' he says sadly, 'there are only pockets of excellence.'

No one knows the exact number of tanneries in Kanpur. It might be 370, it might be 420—some of them operate in secret, some are not even members of the Association of Small Tanneries of Kanpur, an organization representing a hundred thousand jobs, operating out of a garage with false flooring. Tiny tanneries with a courtyard, a roof for the vat, an open space for the drum and a shed for the stretching and polishing of the skin, with thirty workers as poor as the surroundings. In the vats, in a lye of ground bark, water and other components, the skin is marinated over three months. Then it is put into the drum together with special oil and a few chemicals. When the door of the drum is opened, a stinking lye flows on to the ground; the workers wade in it without protection; the skin is hung to dry; the lye drains away, through a gutter into a channel, through a channel into a waste pipe, directly into the Ganges.

In the middle of the courtyard lay the dented half of a car wreck, with two fat geese sauntering around it. A wilful stench permeated everything. The owners showed us around nervously—they probably assumed that we were from some environmental agency. They led us into the shed where a few narrow-chested old men and red-eyed children toiled in unnatural twilight, surrounded by emaciated goats. The children brushed a liquid on to the skins, the old men worked a machine that resembled a medieval torture instrument and seemed to polish the tautly stretched skin. Horror was normality.

'My hobby,' said Imran Siddiqui in his air-conditioned office just a few minutes' walk away, 'is morphology.' He fingered the leaf of a plant on his desk like a diagnosing dermatologist. 'I compare this plant with others that grow two kilometres from here. I note the differences. You would be surprised by the differences.'

In front of his office building we had seen crowded pots and plants—altogether he had gathered more than ten thousand plants and over seven hundred species. A miniature jungle bordered the driveway. Imran Siddiqui, a trained chemical engineer who manages the largest tannery in town, offered us an espresso and asked which beans we preferred, Colombian, Brazilian or Kenyan.

'I also concern myself with the advantages of tanning with vegetable substances. I am on the verge of developing a process that will substantially reduce environmental pollution.'

He pulled thick, neatly catalogued folders out of a cupboard and leafed through coloured print-outs, photocopies, diagrams and tables, sorted by ecological theme. He took out a few pages and pressed the button below his desk, summoning a seventy-year-old peon into whose hands the pages were pushed for copying.

'I am at my desk every morning at five to eight; it sets an example. If someone doesn't turn up for work until five past eight, he is marked absent and has to pay a penalty. Often I stay in the office as late as nine or ten. Then I drive home, have my dinner and settle down in front of the computer, surfing the Net for interesting information, often till one or two in the morning.'

I asked him whether he was a bachelor. He paused briefly before replying, 'No, but I must say I owe everything to my wife's understanding.'

As we said goodbye, Imran Siddiqui—like every successful Kanpurite—gave me two business cards; the second one announced him as Hon. Sec. of the Green Clean People Society.

Rakesh had once more sat beside me silently. 'In Kanpur,' he told me outside, in the midst of abundant greenery, 'everybody tells you how much he cherishes nature. And everybody messes it up without a second thought.'

~

During our last conversation Govind revealed himself as a sceptic who entertained doubts about scepticism.

'Why do I carry this moonstone ring? Because I like it? No way. Cheap stuff. An ordinary setting, fixed up in a jiffy so that I could carry the ring the same day. That was last week. Because someone had advised me to wear a moonstone ring. Why do I, who am educated and have even studied in the US, pay attention to such nonsense? Why? I really have no idea. I was in Delhi a few days ago. There, a friend sent me to a tantrik. It wasn't easy to find him; he roosted in a poky room with a low ceiling in a bad neighbourhood. We exchanged a few pleasantries, then he asked me about my problem. "My daughter," I said. "A suitable boy hasn't shown up yet. One seemed like the right choice, there was a meeting between the two, but he never got in touch again."

'While I was talking, the tantrik scribbled something on a piece of paper.

'"And," he asked, "anything else?"

'"Business isn't doing very well either."

'"Aha."

'He folded the paper to the size of a fingernail and placed it between us on a low table.

'"Tell me a number between 1 and 254."

'"113," I said just like that, it came into my mind.

"'Why 113,' the man asked. "Thirteen is regarded as an unlucky number, and 113 is dangerously close."

"'I don't know why I said 113,' I answered.

"'*Achcha, achcha*,' the sage murmured and threw his writing at me.

'I unfolded the paper and read: "daughter—Yukti, number—113." I was baffled; Yukti is a rare name.

"'Your daughter will marry,' the sage said.

"'When,' I asked him.

'And he said: "Soon, do not worry!"'

~

Govind's wife, Raksha, brought us to the railway station. While we waited for the delayed train to arrive, we drank Pepsi out of plastic cups. The empties stacked in my hand, I searched for a dustbin. 'Just dump them anywhere,' a waiting soldier advised. The platform was covered in blue and red, plastic cups were either crumpled or trampled. I ran up and down, provoked by Raksha's assertion that I would never find a dustbin. I asked at kiosks; each time I was told with an unmistakable gesture that I should throw away the cup, never mind where. Finally, right at the end of the platform, I found a trash barrel—it was empty. I tossed my Pepsi cups into it with a flourish.

The nectar of the masses

Every twelve years Kumbhnagar, the most densely populated fairground on earth, a tentopolis near the city of god, is built on the sandy banks of the Ganges and Yamuna. For the first Maha Kumbh Mela of the twenty-first century, the Uttar Pradesh government divided the grey wasteland at the *Sangam* into twelve sectors. It laid out 450 kilometres of cables and 145 kilometres of water pipes; it paved 140 kilometres of roads, built twenty thousand toilet boxes, erected fifteen pontoon bridges and connected five thousand telephones. The organization was impressive: six thousand garbage men collected the waste; the roads, consolidated with sand sheets, were sprinkled every night; thousands of volunteers maintained daily order.

~

The *kalpavasi* knows he must embark on this *yatra*. Just like his father and his grandfather before him.

He does not spend many thoughts on practicalities—
a kalpavasi is always looked after. He has rarely
travelled beyond the confines of his village, never
beyond the market town. This journey will surpass
all previous experiences. The *zamindar* has made a
tractor available, which pulls the trailer, on which
many families huddle together. The tractor only
stops for the most urgent of human needs. Sleep is
not one of them. During the night the headlights
break down. They only hear the hysterical hooting of
the bus which nearly slams into them. Shortly before
arrival, the voices of those who have undergone this
yatra before flare up. But none of their stories can
prepare the kalpavasi for the sight that opens up in
front of him as the tractor chugs over the Ganges
Bridge in Allahabad.

As far as he can see through the dusty mist, there
are tents on both sides of the river, makeshift wooden
structures, poles and streets as straight as a ruler.
Everything moves: brusque policemen; a procession
of white-clad sadhus; a jeep being hauled out of the
soft sand; an elephant blessing the heads of the

116

kalpavasis with his trunk, and there are many who request this benediction with a coin. Finally they reach their camp: open tents, a canvas cover stretched between two posts. Hardly a defence against the cold. Already occupied by bundles and blankets. After a lot of pleading and urging, everyone finds a place for his plastic bag or his gunny sack. The women start cooking: dough is kneaded, rolled out, the chapattis prepared. The *pujari* from their village temple announces that they will take *snaan* early next morning.

On the opposite river bank, a handful of sadhus are singing inside a small, inhabited temple. The Nestor of the group plays the harmonium, his face the faded print of an ancient icon. He is accompanied on the *tabla* by a young ascetic with a Trotsky beard, next to whom sits a jester, plump as a laughing Buddha. The other sadhus clap with their cymbals and evoke in a single voice the name of the divine couple *Sita-Ram*. Over microphone and a quavering loudspeaker, the singing reaches out. The sadhus have found a realm in which they would like to abide forever. The ancient song sounds as fresh as if it were being sung for the very first time. Outside of the song everything falls apart. Plastic sheets offer privacy, a piece of corrugated iron—not large enough—serves as the roof. One of the walls has collapsed a long time ago, patched up with bricks that have lasted as long as they could. In place of windows, holes have been punched into the walls. In the ante-room of the *mandir*, a toothless crone and her daughter have furnished a makeshift home.

The song of the sadhus comes to an end. The plump jester is talked into a solo. He draws his orange cloth like a wimple over his head. Faster and faster he whirls to the sounds of a coquette song, grimacing and clowning. The other sadhus accompany him with clapping and laughter. A last pirouette, then he freezes, as if he had taken an overdose of opium. The women rise and present him, after a drum-whirl of gestures, with rupee notes. The jester drowns the notes in a fold of his shawl and steps back into a choir that is oblivious to sleep.

~

Every morning we wake up to the screech of 108 godly names; our alarm clock is a suffocating mist of song and sound, our dawn full of clanking crickets. Incantations, each prayer besieged by a multitude of competing prayers. No holiness, no solidarity, no inwardness, no mercy. Only noise. And the loudest of all mantras, the ultimate destroyer of sleep—*Shanti om!*

The naked initiates, whose heads (except for the *kuthumi*) have been tonsured three days ago, squat on the banks of the Ganges, in rank and file, as if they were representing their regiment at a parade. Behind them, a few festively dressed sadhus swagger, after vacating a piece of the bank with loud words and threatening gestures from other pilgrims. An elderly man, carelessly coming too close, is chased away with a brandishing stick. The *sadhu* commandants shout orders for every single step of the initiation. They shoo the candidates into the water and hail them back to shore, they have them squat and stand, step back, squat and stand. A *Tata Sumo* drives up, a general steps out, dressed up as a highly revered *guru*.

119

The master of ceremonies, dressed in a red brocade robe and a triumphant turban, wades through the shallow water, swinging a long silver stick in front of the naked ranks and pours a handful of *Gangajal* over each proffered skull. The aspirants hold out both arms. Then they plunge in groups into the river and frolic. After the bath they run, jump and hop like unbridled children in the knee-deep water. Finally they are presented with a white *langoti*, which they tie around their waist; their discarded underpants flow on with the current towards Kolkata (formerly Calcutta). They have been initiated as sadhus.

Not all of them follow a spiritual course. Some escape from rural poverty into the social security of the thirteen *akharas*, the paramilitary organizations into which the sadhus are grouped; some are refugees from the law; others are ill in spirit—as holy fools, the sadhus have always been accorded care and respect. In the camps of the sadhus you find fanatics and academics, quacks and romantics. They sit in front of their tents near the permanently burning holy fire, allowing the believers to worship them with looks, touches and donations; substantial heaps of money are piled up in from of them. A peasant touches the sole of a *sadhu*, weeping bitterly. The *sadhu* listens, caressing with one hand a beautiful black dog. Sadhus give advice, they chase bad spirits away with a whisk of their peacock feather, they press a pinch of *vibhuti* on to lines of worry. Some wear nothing besides their malas. For the sadhus the mela is a meeting and market place, a holiday resort, a political stage—a temporary diversion from meditation.

The akharas were founded about a thousand years ago, in disquieting times of inner disintegration and Muslim threat. Since then they have offered instruction in *shastra* (holy text) and *shaastra* (weapons). The militant attributes—in the middle of the camp, an amazing variety of spears and other stabbing weapons were rammed into the ground—symbolize their worldly might. Some sadhus are believed to have the powers of medicine men, magicians or shamans. Those who have taken oaths of penance command special reverence. An elderly *sadhu* has become a media star because he has been holding up his completely withered arm for more than a decade. A young brother in faith from Varanasi has stood for three years, day and night, on one leg; nine more years await him. With one leg in life, just like the goddess *Mrityu*, who refused to obey *Brahma*'s order to bring death into the world and protested by remaining on one leg for fifteen million years. An unperturbed *Brahma* just reminded her of her duty. She changed legs and protested for another twenty million years. But that also failed to change *Brahma*'s mind—finally death was introduced into the world.

Our grey-haired neighbour in the camp is an NRI psychiatrist from Kentucky, who speaks with a drawl. For ten years, he says, he has been trying to build up a spiritual life, using Hindu concepts of mind and consciousness in his therapy, which translates practically into the use of meditation techniques and yoga. He is amused by the tense seriousness of the US-American neo-Hindus, who arrive in large groups and devote themselves to the holy festival for a couple of streamlined days.

'They want to achieve quick results in anything they do. Look at their daily schedule: two hours of yoga, breakfast, four hours of *yagna*, lunch, two hours of satsang, tea break, one hour of *aarti*, an hour of leisure, supper, then meditation or a lecture. A day fit for a competitive athlete. They seem to be training for the Olympics of Salvation. I'm sure you know the story of the shishya who asks his *guru*: "How long will it take for me to achieve liberation?"

"A whole life," the *guru* answers.

"And if I try very hard?"

"Several lives!"

"But what if I give it all I have?"

"Then you will never attain it!"'

At supper I am seated next to one of these athletes of spirituality, a heavy-boned and heavy-fleshed man from Minnesota, who does the cliché of his origin justice by looking exactly like a Viking. He speaks in measured tones, without doubt impressed by the omnipresent authenticity, 'When I took my bath this morning, I felt the power of god entering my body and cleansing me of all worries.'

His words sound like a well-prepared statement to the press. We are sitting cross-legged on the floor and eating chawal, dal, sabzi and chapatti with our fingers out of a palm-leaf plate.

'It seems to me,' the man continues gravely, 'that nowhere in the world are people as innocent as they are here, as innocent perhaps as they once were everywhere on this planet, before capitalism destroyed everything. I am aware of the poverty and the destitution; nevertheless, India is still innocent!'

After supper we wash our hands in a big wooden tub. I meet the psychiatrist for a cigarette in the frosty night wind, while the American rushes off to learn correct breathing techniques.

'US society,' the psychiatrist remarks, 'is insecure, people lack self-confidence. In India, however, people are buoyed up by a primal faith due to their ancient religious traditions. This faith breeds self-esteem, a self-esteem I myself feel whenever I come home to India. In the USA this self-confidence is diminishing, as if encircled, surrounded by others. That is the problem. Once you lose your primal faith, you cannot win it back.'

A pit littered with *chai* cups, some made of plastic, now crushed and crumpled, others made of clay, already dissolving under the dew. In the small pit, old and new lie next to one another, mixed and intermingled; the ancient is about to pass away, while the modern is geared for eternity, or at least for a *kalpa* which seems to us eternal. It is Mauni Amavasya, the most important of the four days of holy *snaan*, and amidst the burgeoning masses the concept of eternity seems positively frightening. At four o'clock in the morning, the dust of many paths is whirled up by innumerable feet on their way to the *Sangam*. One of the pontoon bridges is reserved for the carnival of the akharas. The gurus of the gurus are enthroned like kings on richly adorned carts, followed by their foot soldiers. Lesser sadhus hold sunshades over the mahants. In waves the akharas flow towards the river, gigantic banners sailing in the fresh morning wind. The human mass seems to stand still, but, at the edges, behind the provisional fences, it frays out to shoving and jostling. People are waiting for *darshan*.

The kalpavasis can no longer be counted. Observers make nebulous guesses—eleven, twenty-two or maybe thirty-three million. Policemen patrol along the wooded fence, swinging their batons as mercilessly as hedge-cutters. Old sadhus hold each other's hands, trembling. After the *snaan* they rub themselves with *vibhuti*, which they have brought along in plastic bags, until the shivering subsides. 'This water is truth,' one of them shouts. 'God is in us, but we are not aware of him—this *snaan* makes us remember God's presence!'

Loudspeakers proclaim the end of the allotted time. Policemen thrash half-dressed bathers, who are desperately trying to heave a second foot into their trousers. Old women, both hands struggling to bind their saris, are defenceless against the heavy blows.

Dawn light reveals a battle scene. The marching up of the Juna Akhara, the most militant of akharas. A vanguard of two *naga* sadhus on beautifully decorated horses: one holding the banner, the other beating a hard rhythm. Serpentine trumpets and trishuls rise out of the formation of a thousand *naga* sadhus. With coarse yells they run through the sand, they fly down the dunes and into the river, hopping over the water, splashing each other.

After the bath the *naga* sadhus swing swords, their wet skin glistening in the morning sun. One of the brigade snatches the camera of a foreign journalist and throws it on to the ground, spearing it with a trishul as if it were a demon. A comrade accompanies him in an ecstatic dance over the conquered camera. A clothed *sadhu* catches everything on Betacam. On the other side of the spit, a photo session is in progress. Sadhus are modelling, climbing a fence, posing, showing off their muscles like bodybuilders in a contest. They shower the assembled photographers with abuse and vulgar gestures. A policeman throws stones at the photographers. A *sadhu* throws pebbles at the policeman. There is panic amongst the naked and the clothed as the sadhus make their way back to camp. A *sadhu* climbs on to the fence and vigorously calls the other sadhus to order, a threatening trishul in his hand. The warlike attitude slips off; the *naga* sadhus retreat like frightened children. Soon the whole pontoon bridge is covered with bodies. An army of naked saints bridges *Ganga* mataji.

～

Early in the morning dense fog has swallowed all. Kumbhnagar seems to have dissolved in Brahman. In the unseen all elements are linked with one another. The senses are as transient as the human, and the individual is just a fleeting chimera on the dusty road from nothing to nothing. Only the loudspeakers are oblivious to the reality of transition and passage. They wail through the fog, they will continue to wail, even when there is nothing more to be seen.

Confluences

Those who bathe in the confluence of the white and dark rivers will ascend to heaven.

On the last evening of the Kumbh Mela, a bitterly cold evening, we were strolling through the endless rows of tents when the surprise of an unexpected song attracted us to an open tent. Some twenty sadhus were comfortably seated on the floor, completely immersed in the performance of a group of singers.

They invited us to join them. At the end of the song, which we listened to with growing bewilderment, they greeted us politely.

'But wasn't that a qawwali,' I asked, impatient in my surprise.

'Yes, yes,' the sadhus replied joyfully, shaking their long-haired and long-bearded heads.

'How come you are listening to qawwali, here at the Kumbh Mela?'

Now it was the turn of the sadhus to be perplexed. 'It brings us closer to god—that's why!'

In India such mixtures of religious forms can be found nearly everywhere. They have led to an ongoing formation of syncretistic beliefs, to the metamorphosis of the great religions as well as to the birth of new cults. The followers of one of these new religions perform their central pilgrimage in Panna, a district town a few hours drive south-west of Allahabad, in the middle of wild Bundelkhand, a land of tigers, waterfalls and ruins that the jungle has reclaimed. In this town, early in the morning, thousands of men and women go marching to the surrounding hills in great haste to surpass the rising sun. At the main crossroads of the town, raggedly dressed people hope to be hired for a daily wage of Rs 70 by those who can afford to acquire digging rights. Half the population has already searched for diamonds; a few of them have been rewarded with glittering villas on the slope that was once home to the local magistrate of the British Empire.

At first glance the temple that we had come to see could not be assigned to any particular religion. The exterior with its multitude of cupolas and arches was reminiscent of a gurudwara; the inner walls were lined with pictures of Krishna, but there were only a flute and a crown on a finely embroidered cushion in the sanctum sanctorum. The crown was inlaid with precious stones, among them a ruby as large as a cherry. On the opposite wall was the portrait of a man in the mudra of blessing, introduced by the lettering on the frame as Lord Prannath; he wore the beard typical of a devout Muslim. In a corridor we saw a plump baby, recoloured by computer as a Krishna icon. The picture's pastel colours were repeated on the yellow, green and pink pillars. The believers, in their gestures of worship less eclectic than the building itself, greeted one another with a loud '*pranam*'.

The temple was the Mecca and Vrindavan of the Pranami, a sect that accepts all religions and recognizes all saints and prophets as messengers of god in an effort to pave the way for a universal religion. Mahamati Prannath, their bearded prophet, was a Gujarati, born in 1618 in Jamnagar; his father had served as a minister at the court of the local ruler, and his uncle had been a diamond trader in Arabia. In those days a sizeable number of affluent and respected Arabs lived in the trading cities of the Kathiawar peninsula. Mahamati Prannath seems to have learnt Arabic and studied the Koran intensively. He travelled through the Arab region for almost a decade, living in Basra, Muscat, Koga and Bandar Abbas. At that time he already preached that god was one and formless and that all religions worshipped this one and only god. There is no record that he was tortured or persecuted even once during his journeys on account of his preaching. Two and a half centuries later, in Porbander, a mere hundred kilometres away from Jamnagar, a boy was born whose father served the local ruler as a minister. His family also belonged to the Pranami sect. As a man he was to spend much of his life pleading for the reconciliation of Hindus and Muslims. As a boy he grew up with rituals during which the priest recited from the Koran as well as from the *Bhagavadgita*, shifting from one to the other as if it made no difference from which book he read as long as he was worshipping god. However, in the official hagiography this early religious conditioning of *Mahatma* Gandhi hardly finds mention.

An old man sat in a corner of the temple and read from the holy book *Kuljam Sharif* (fourteen volumes containing 18,758 verses, including texts from different religions along with references). A loudspeaker broadcast his voice across the entire temple area.

'Day and night someone reads from this book. Our belief does not allow us to convert people,' the priest explained. 'It is necessary to change one's own spiritual attitude. As long as one understands one's religion correctly, it does not matter to which religion one belongs. Conflicts originate in the ignorance of people and are rooted in external differences. This is the cause of all the world's misery. When they have understood this, they will realize that there is only one religion that can exist in this world and that is the religion of god and that only one people that can exist on this earth—the people of god.'

These commandments were sufficient, the priest evidently believed, to resolve all religious conflicts. However, his temple was empty and the city in which Lord Prannath had obtained enlightenment had caught diamond fever. The voice of the toothless old man echoed through lonely marble rooms. The priest presented me with a brochure, printed in Allahabad and bound with rusty clips, which proudly informed the reader that Lord Prannath had deserved mention in *The Cambridge History of India*. Just one line though.

On our last evening in Allahabad we ate at Spicy Bite on M.G. Road. Our waiter was a dark-skinned man who dragged his right foot. He took our orders silently and then said in excellent English, 'You live in India, you speak good Hindi.'

That was all he said, adding a sentence or two every time he came to serve us. He stood apart from the other waiters on account of his multicoloured candy shirt, whose short sleeves he had rolled up as if he wanted to show off his biceps. This did not match his watchful, sad gaze.

'And you,' we asked, 'where did you learn English?'

'In school and in films. I was in Bombay for two years. I played the villain because my face is so dark.' He laughed dryly and advised us to order a certain dish, before dragging himself to the next table.

'People call me "Bombaya" now,' he said, our drinks in his hand. 'I acted on the stage here in Allahabad, I sang Bollywood numbers. Then I went to Bombay.'

His friends had encouraged him at the time: You can make it in Bollywood! You really have it in you!

He served the tandoori chicken and the cheese paratha. 'I shot two films—*Bombay 405 Miles* and *Kranti*. Then my boss died of a heart attack.'

We started eating, with one leg in a traffic jam,

pestered by business-hungry rickshaw drivers and blind beggars accompanied by children.

'Do you want to order something more?'

We declined, but I asked him why he had come back from Mumbai.

'I came away because there is no friendship there. When one is sick, when one is feeling miserable, one is alone there.' He cleared the table and soon came back with the bill. 'There was no other job for me here in Allahabad. So I work here, for the last ten years. But if there is a chance, if someone wanted me there, I would immediately return to Bombay. Even if I had to leave my family and friends back here.'

Breathing with the soles

Yours is a journey without aim
for you have already arrived.

The sandbanks on the confluence of the Ganges and Jamuna showed no signs of human existence. I closed my eyes and opened them again, cautiously. Still no sign of human existence. On the bridge a truck wheezed like a man suffering from an allergy;

below, white sand stretched out where a short while ago Kumbhnagar, the city of millions, had stretched out. Only the boatmen remained unchanged—wily and wheedling. During the Kumbh Mela they had publicly complained about the scarcity of pilgrims who were willing to charter a boat. Now they bragged about the excellent business during the festival and demanded peak pilgrim-season rates. They prompted us to throw an offering into the confluence, a five-rupee coin for example. When we were gone, they would dive in to retrieve the offering and salvage not only coins but also coconuts, rings or other pieces of jewellery. The coconuts were cleaned and sold to the next pilgrim; the jewellery was reintroduced into the cycle of monetary economy. In January, I had entered the water without a second thought—full of faith in the Ganges. Now I found it impossible to overcome the memories of the drainage pipes and the gutters of Gajraula, Kanpur and Mirzapur, and I experienced a crisis of belief in the company of three old sadhus who had helped the boatman to drive up the price. In such cases there is only one solution:

fight. I vehemently accused the boatman of cheating and the sadhus of lying; they reacted with supreme disinterest, as if I were reciting the Bulgarian national anthem. It was a relief to reach the southern bank, to fasten our backpacks and to start hiking along the raised embankment; two well-equipped imitators of the age-old tradition of *padayatra*, the pilgrimage on foot.

Only those who witness village life from a distance can exalt it. In Lavan, in the main village square, we asked where we could spend the night and were immediately surrounded by stark and empty gazes (many of the irises were like crushed maggots). The bodies had not been spared either; they had carried too many heavy pots to the well, they had bent too often to plant a seed, they had crushed too many boulders to pebbles and too many pebbles to gravel.

'The Raymond factory has a guest house,' said one.

'No, no,' intervened another, 'these foreigners want to stay here in the village.'

We agreed. A third one then took us by the hand, walked with us barely thirty steps and pointed towards a two-storeyed, fairly large house, apparently the dwelling of a man of status, a rural haveli. We were asked to deposit our luggage on the *charpoy* in front of the house. Women came out and led us into the house. They showed us our bed, just behind the entrance.

We were lodged in the house of the *sarpanch* who zoomed in on a motorbike a few minutes later and greeted us heartily as if he was accustomed to finding foreigners with large backpacks in his house. He was a small, soft-spoken gentleman who changed his clothes quickly before joining us in his lungi and banian. His wealth, he said, was modest. He owned eight buffaloes that he milked himself every morning, and land, on the other side of the road to Mirzapur, on which rice was grown. Everything about him was an understatement; it would have been easy to underestimate him. He would not have stood out in a group of villagers. His importance was emphasized by others in the course of the evening over which he held court. Every few minutes someone would come forward to seek his advice, convey some news to him, demand his help. He listened patiently to each and every one, but said little. He was the sponge that absorbed the problems of the village and sometimes, perhaps, wiped them away. Later, when it was time to retire, he said, 'Go now!' And all those concerned rose immediately and disappeared.

As the sun went down, more and more men gathered in the courtyard of the *sarpanch*'s house. We exchanged pleasantries before discussing practical issues (the way to Diha, the distance to Sirsa). Only after nightfall did we start to talk about life in Uttar Pradesh and in Germany.

The *sarpanch* belonged to the sub-caste of Yadavs, a caste that has earned a lot of money and respect in recent times in this part of India. The caste is represented by the Samajwadi Party, to which the *sarpanch* also belonged (he was astonished when I asked about his party affiliation; it was unthinkable that he should be a member of any other party). The demographic advantage had brought this party to power in many municipalities and even in the state government. The village had elected him as *sarpanch* twice, a post held for a period of five years.

'And what is the cost of milk in Germany?' He seemed to find milk very reasonable, meat quite expensive, beer unbelievably cheap and motorcycles horrendously expensive.

The algebra of politics in this village was simple. The Yadavs as well as the other lower castes numbered several thousands; the Brahmins a mere three hundred and the Dalits six hundred. As a result, the other parties hardly stood a chance against the Samajwadi Party.

'Do you have a caste system in Germany?'

My narration about the abolition of aristocracy was met with great interest.

How did the *sarpanch* earn his living? On weekdays he rode every morning at nine on his motorcycle to the telephone exchange in the vicinity where he earned a salary of Rs 10,000, a small fortune, per month for a comfortable job.

'The caste system will change, slowly, very slowly but surely. One day it will not be of any significance.' The man who said this, most probably a younger brother of the *sarpanch*, spoke with great confidence.

All the men who had gathered there belonged to a self-confident middle class that need not fear comparison with its surroundings, quite unlike the middle class in the cities which is daily confronted with what it lacks. The traditional reference system was still intact; they had experienced a change in the distribution of wealth and power in their favour, and they were well pleased.

At around eight, we were invited to take part in an *aarti*. A pocket torch led us to a temple, a simple structure, open on three sides. Pillars supported the wooden roof; only the sanctum sanctorum had walls. Simple temples have something moving about them. A candle and a paraffin lamp illuminated the moment, the singers were silhouettes, sitting cross-legged on the floor. The singing stroked the night with calloused hands. No refinement was cultivated here. In the darkness of the night, only the direct expression of the voices existed. The *puja* was reduced to the bare minimum, words and tones. It was reminiscent of the old Vedic conception that the gods were put together from verses in metre. When

141

metre was knotted with metre, to a sloka precise in intonation and cadence, the divine became manifest. And so the Brahmins recite the slokas for years, until they have become one with them. The singing was supplemented by the only ritual act of the evening: the rotation of the oil lamp in front of the four idols (the light did not suffice to identify them). An oil lamp, three rotations, very simple. Even the slightest ornament would have disturbed the encounter with the divine. There was no need to explain the spirituality of the moment; it was uplifted and blessed with that which theology so painfully lacks: vitality. At the end of the *aarti*, the curtains of the shrine were drawn and the lights were put out. The gods went to sleep, the people went to eat.

~

The next day we witnessed the birth of a goat kid on the banks of the Ganges. We were stroking the smeared skin of the newborn when a dark man joined us and asked us if he could carry our luggage. He was half my size, his head clean-shaven. He lifted my backpack with one hand and claimed that it was not heavy. It took a while for him to talk us into giving him work. He heaved the backpack, which weighed almost thirty kilos, on to his head, held it with one hand and set off—barefoot. Seemingly effortless.

We tried to stay close to the shore wherever possible; otherwise our journey took us criss-cross through fields and villages, through yards and past houses, accompanied by children, followed by the barking of suspicious dogs. Bijul, for that was the name of the porter, ran behind us. He belonged to one of the lower castes, the Mallahs (boatmen), and his father's name was Gangaram. Whenever we approached a village, a throng of questions followed hard on his heels. He was free with information, although he knew about us only what he had picked up in passing. It was hot and humid. It rained once. We huddled with twenty farmers under the eaves of a hut. We looked out into the rain, the farmers stared at us. It wasn't possible to slot the scene into a specific era.

Bijul grew increasingly self-confident. He took over the role of a manager.

'Where are you heading?' he asked.

'To Mirzapur.'

'Okay, I am coming along.'

After a few kilometres he asked again, 'And after Mirzapur, where to?'

'Varanasi.'

'Okay, I am coming along to Varanasi.'

'And after Varanasi?' he inquired some time later as if an idea had suddenly struck him.

'Patna, Bihar.'

'Okay, I am coming along till Patna.'

'And after Patna?' he asked at our next halt.

'Calcutta.'

'Oh! I am coming with you to Calcutta.'

A *sadhu* stopped and greeted us. 'Where does the road take you?'

'To Mirzapur.'

'Where from?'

'From Allahabad.'

'By foot?'

'Yes, a padayatra, always along the shore.'

'Very good!' The *sadhu*'s face lit up. 'Very good.'

No more questions about significance and intention. The word padayatra held all answers.

We walked a few kilometres through a desolate alluvial plain, warned by everyone on the way to beware of robbers. Bijul walked ahead and sang *'Namahashivay, om Namahashivay, om Namahashivay, om Namahashivay.'* He sometimes alternated the hand that balanced the backpack on his head and sang *'Sita Ram, Sita Ram, Sita Ram, Ram, Ram'* for a change. The robbers stayed out of sight.

We reached the Tons river at sunset. While we were waiting for a boat, Bijul announced that he had a sister in Sirsa with whom we could stay and asked if we approved. We looked forward to it. Two women, two children and one man got out of the solitary ferry boat. The women, dressed in their finest saris, high-heeled shoes, manicured in garish colours, covered with jewellery, stepped carefully into the muddy earth.

'Where to?'

'To the village,' said the man.

'But the next village is several kilometres away, isn't it?'

'Yes, only one hour,' said the man cheerfully and shouldered his youngest daughter.

The ferryman knew Bijul, and they gabbled away. Bijul suddenly asked about the bus connection from Sirsa, the village we were fast approaching, to Mirzapur. I was momentarily astonished, but didn't pay much attention to the question.

At his sister's house, Bijul did not receive any visible welcome. He entered the house as if he had never been away. He introduced us to his sister only when we insisted. We greeted her; silhouettes of children appeared on the balustrade of the roof, one after the other. I counted aloud up to nine. 'Nine children,' I said jokingly to the sister.

'No,' she said without batting an eyelid, 'I have eight children.'

We sat on a *charpoy* in front of the house, surrounded by people numberless in the twilight. Bijul fanned me with a reed-stringed bamboo frame resembling an antique tennis racket, his sister fanned Pac. An uncomfortable colonial moment that we ended with the lie that we were not feeling hot.

Bijul had suddenly fallen silent; his self-confidence, which had grown during our long march until he had completely discarded his initial servility, evaporated within minutes. He asked quietly if we were interested in going to the bazaar with a few friends of his, without mentioning that we would have to walk another two kilometres in total darkness. We reached a tea-stall where the boys sat down with as much excitement as if this was their regular pub. We drank a very sweet *chai* and marched back two kilometres. Meanwhile I was dreaming of cable cars, or at least a wheelchair. Back in the bosom of the family, Bijul was loudly admonished, but we didn't understand why. He just imploded without a word. The only possibility of taking a bath was at a public water pump. Unfortunately the power supply was back; the slanting light served an attentive audience well.

It was a pity that Pac had not mastered the art of bathing with her clothes on. I had to shield her with a hand towel. I kept changing my position, raising and lowering the towel, in a game of skill against the voyeurism of the villagers. In the middle of the night, we were awakened by full-throated chanting just outside our door.

'*Namahashivay, om namahashivay.*'

Bijul lay outside on the *charpoy*. After a few minutes, I could tolerate it no longer.

'Bijul,' I said, 'don't you want to sleep?'

'*Namahashivay, om namahashivay.*'

'Bijul,' I shouted, 'we cannot sleep because of your chanting.'

'*Namahashivay, om namahashivay.*'

'Bijul,' I roared, 'shut up!' The night sank at last into silence.

The next morning Bijul suggested that we take the bus to Mirzapur.

'No, Bijul, we want to go on foot.'

'But it is much more comfortable by bus.'

'Bijul, we are doing a padayatra. And anyway, what will you do if we take the bus?'

'I must go back to my village, I must go back to my village because of my family!'

He didn't want to say more despite our persistent questioning. We clicked the obligatory family photograph, noted down the address of our hosts and left unaccompanied on our onward journey. We reached the main road in the afternoon, exhausted, and travelled the remaining kilometres to Mirzapur by bus.

The fabled town of carpets

On a pavement in Mirzapur lay a dead horse, dramatically collapsed, one eye reproachfully fixed on the Sunday strollers, as if Franz Marc had suffered a heart attack while painting. A few rats scuttered across the street. The town was worn out, the houses ruins, as if refugees survived in them, hiding behind heaps of rubbish. The painted back of a rickshaw helped us make our peace with the traffic jam: a river, two leisurely crocodiles, palm trees along the banks, swallows in the air and a sun on a flying carpet. A carpet of silk and cotton, woven in one of the workshops we were passing, by children's fingers that would never break a toy. On reaching Hotel Jahnvi, the rickshaw-wallah demanded Rs 500, then 300, then 100, propelled down this rapid fall by my crazed laugh. The receptionist suggested that the correct price was around Rs 35. The rickshaw-wallah refused to accept the fifty-rupee note I held out to him. The manager rebuked him, 'Tourists don't visit Mirzapur because of people like you!' He spoke from experience. We were the only guests in his hotel; the mineral water was served either warm or frozen. The posters on the wall were courtesy of the Uttar Pradesh Tourism Board, pictures of the Ganges in Caribbean masquerade, invitations to a sightseeing tour on a flying carpet. From our balcony we could see *Ganga* turning her back on this town.

The room was as large as a garage, and as dimly lit, surprisingly enough, for the underage boys standing in front of us, smiling shyly, had to weave elaborate designs with their thin, nimble fingers. It hadn't been easy to find a workshop open on Sunday. We inquired with some passers-by; a man approached us, his face assembled from second-hand parts. A desperately chewing jaw accentuated the disorder of his features. Reddish liquid trickled from one side of his mouth, as if he were impersonating *Kali* from a particularly gory reproduction. We could hardly understand him. *'Mushkil,'* he seemed to mutter, *'mushkil.'* He drove us in a brand new *Tata Sumo* to a luxurious house. 'My uncle,' he seemed to mumble. His uncle was relaxing on the veranda, clad in a shrunken undershirt, the hairs on his belly crawling like tame earthworms. A bamboo scaffold, sacks of sand and the loud diligence of a few workers surrounded him. He raised himself up with heavy idleness, put on a shirt and started buttoning it up, while chatting with the *paan*-chewer. He paused to chuck a few rough orders at the workers. The two men glanced at us several times. The chat ended at the last button, which was left undone. The uncle disappeared into the house; we were driven back to the place from where we had been picked up. Hardly ten steps away, the man lifted a plastic sheet and pointed towards the garage-sized workshop. 'The young man will help you,' he said in farewell. 'He is my son.'

With his twenty years, the son seemed like an elderly, experienced manager beside the workers

151

whose voices had not yet broken. All the walls were covered with unfinished carpets, in the corners rolls piled up. Supple and nimble fingers are supposed to be a professional advantage: children are cheap and powerless. 'We look after them,' the young manager retorted. 'They know nothing, they are good for nothing, we teach them, we give them a room, we feed them and clothe them. What else would they do? Their parents can't afford to send them to school, and there are no other industries around here. Don't you want to see our carpets? Mirzapur survives on carpets.'

Kneeling down I viewed a few kilims with designs which were threaded in Persia four centuries ago, abstractions of beauty and suffering. The manager, mistaking my silence for fascination, rolled out one carpet after the other. It was stuffy and humid in the garage, sweat was dripping from my forehead on to the carpets. I stood up quickly and collided with one of the boys, who stumbled. In a reflex I held him upright; a bag of bones and an impish smile.

'Our prices are low,' I heard the young, efficient manager proclaim. 'In any shop in Delhi or Bombay you would pay several times the amount. Only high quality, just turn it over.'

In the world of carpets free trade reigns supreme and the flip side unmasks the artwork as underpaid drudgery. The Chinese, latecomers, have flooded the market with dirt-cheap machine-made products. The workshops in India, Pakistan and Iran cannot afford mechanization; the knots continue to be tied by scrawny children's fingers. And the prices are kept competitive by cutting the costs of this labour.

We had barely left the factory when a *Tata Sumo* stopped next to us and one of the doors opened. First we heard someone spitting and then an invitation to get in. The *paan*-chewer sat on the front seat next to driver, along with a girl. 'My daughter,' he said immediately as introduction; behind him sat a few people who might have been his relatives, but who were certainly not cut from the same features.

'Where are we going?' I asked after a while.

'For a picnic,' he mumbled back.

'We would like to go to the Vindhyachal temple, we don't have much time,' I said.

'Oh, *Kali*! You like *Kali*.' The red teeth grinned at us. 'Bad stories, bad place.'

The four-wheel drive swerved about and we raced through the city.

'Many human sacrifices for *Kali*.'

The vehicle resolutely hooted all rickshaws out of the way. 'Not with knife, not with gun.'

A policeman forced the vehicle to stop at a crossing. The *paan*-chewer drew out a handkerchief, turned towards us, dangled it in front of our surprised eyes.

'This thing brought death,' he said. 'The handkerchief was *Kali*'s weapon,' and he started laughing like an exploding cracker.

When we stopped again, he got off and came back with ten wrapped paans and laid them out— his provisions for the afternoon. He decided genially to elaborate on his obscure hints. '*Kali* was the goddess of some bandits, they were called Thugs. Sometimes *Kali* is good, sometimes *Kali* is evil.'

At the next crossing he tied a knot into his handkerchief.

'When evil became weak, *Kali* came to the rescue of the Thugs.'

He tied the handkerchief round his neck and pulled it firmly, his red tongue hung out of his mouth, his eyes bulged, everybody in the car laughed. 'Today the bandits are only petty thieves. They are not even worshippers of *Kali*, just thieves. Times are bad.'

The Thugs, the bandits of yore who strangled their victims with knotted handkerchiefs, played havoc in the Gangetic plains for centuries. Every year they strangled at least thirty thousand travellers, according to the estimates of the British authorities at the beginning of the nineteenth century. They offered a part of their booty to the Vindhyachal shrine, which we were now approaching at snail's pace. For a *mandir* the floor was unexpectedly dirty; the pujaris especially blatant. Only one rupee, they proclaimed, as if they were offering cucumbers rather than blessings. When one of them tugged expectantly at my sleeve, I turned around and snapped, 'Since when does god need money?'

He stroked his belly and answered, 'I need money.'

Since he seemed to be pretty well-fed and had stuck three coins in his ear, I stood in the queue for the *darshan* without paying him any further attention. Somebody shouted *Jai Vindhyachal* (Long live the Goddess), others picked up the chant. That was the cry the Thugs uttered to bid the world goodbye before they were hanged. The paunchy men around me held on to their offerings, bowed at the first step, stroked the wet floor with two fingers and then striped their foreheads. The devotion soon gave way to pushy impatience. The man behind me jostled me many times although the queue was still long. I turned my head and shouted euphorically like a devotee, 'Jai Vindhyachal', in the naive hope that the man would be silenced by my piety. He gave me a punch in the back in answer, and I swung my elbows back in retaliation. He complained, I could feel his breath on my back. I turned around and showered him with a tirade about the value of patience in general and in particular. The man shook his head and stared at his hands. When I gasped for breath, he screeched, '*Chalo*, move on'.

The queue slowly crept into the sanctum sanctorum, a neon-lit cavern. In the corridor, separated from the idol by a grill, each pilgrim was caught between shoving and retreating. Behind the grill a *pujari* leant against the wall, a satiated predator. The other pujaris reacted to the swelling panic in a routine way with lathi blows and well-judged shoves. The two pujaris next to the idol had the toughest job. The offerings of the pilgrims, handed over through the grill, were collected in a fluid movement with half a turn of the body, laid on a ledge before the idol, left alone for a split-second blessing, while the next offering was accepted and laid on the ledge, after which the first one was picked up and passed back to the devotee through the grill. The *pujari* at the exit, sceptical about the visitor's insight into the necessity of urgency, jostled every devotee briskly out. The idol that I saw in the single second granted to me appeared to be cute rather than terrifying: a prominent dark nose (Bhagwan Bhawani, Dark Mother, is the name of this goddess), silver eyes and a red mouth. The rest of the face and body was covered with garlands, cloth and a glittering crown. One last well-meaning push and I tumbled into the courtyard breathing a sigh of relief.

We could not find the way out and asked a *pujari* for help; he nodded in a friendly manner, led us round three corners before stopping in front of an orange-painted *Ganesh* and asked for a donation. 'You are nothing but a Thug reborn,' I said in a language he did not understand.

He smiled back.

'Jai Vindhyachal,' I shouted.

He repeated the call and pocketed the coins I offered him. I was reminded of an old Chinese proverb: When you are forced to do something, just relax and enjoy it.

Life is death is life is death

Gorakh was yoga's connoisseur.
They didn't cremate
his body.
Still his body rotted and mixed

with dust. For nothing
he polished his body.

The foreigners are led in groups to the Manikarnika *Ghat*.

'Here burning *ghat*!' the guide starts his speech with these matter-of-fact words. 'These fires burn day and night, you know. Hindus are burnt here after death, but not all corpses are allowed, okay. No babies, pregnant women, sadhus, lepers, no one dead of smallpox, no chicken pox, no cobra bites, okay. These are wrapped in cloth, a stone is tied to the corpse, then thrown into the river.'

The tourists watch the five burning pyres from the dress circle of a temple yard.

'This fire is burning since times immemorial, okay, it takes three hours for the corpse to burn.'

Handkerchiefs are held to cover nose and mouth.

'Some simple wood, some sandalwood so that it smells good, some *ghee* so that it burns well.'

The tourist group huddles up closer.

'Not everything gets burnt, okay, the rest, the

pelvis, hip of women, chest of men, thrown into *Ganga* river.'

Some of the tourists can no longer face this much reality.

'Women are not allowed here, okay, too emotional, start to cry; just two years ago a widow threw herself into the fire.'

The guide explains that their next stop would be the nearby *Kashi Karvat Mandir*; he knows when the tourists have had enough. Sometimes he omits the story of the suicide pilgrims who threw themselves on to a broadsword sunk into the floor of this temple. The voyeurs move on, some relieved, others smug at having outsmarted the ban on photography. If they had stood there to watch death a little longer, they could have seen how the *doms*, the professional corpse-burners, stoked the ashes to find the jewellery that pious husbands leave on their departed wives.

Time and again travel guides and travelogues peddle the myth that death is omnipresent in Varanasi. Welcome to the city of death, to which every Hindu goes to die! It is true that pilgrims regard Varanasi,

160

the oldest city in India, as a metaphysical site par excellence. But, in reality, the people of Varanasi are remarkable for their joie de vivre. The 125,000 looms of the city do not weave shrouds (a blend of cotton and silk, explains the guide, embroidered with the name of god), but artfully ornamented silk saris for weddings and other joyous occasions. The weavers are all Muslims, who also take a bath in the Ganges but certainly are not cremated. The city's many music schools do not rehearse Indian requiems (there is no scope for such romantic sorrow), but the *sa re ga ma pa da ni sa* of life affirmation and it is well worth the pandits' time. They know that the foreigners, attracted by transcendental fragrances, are in a hurry so they capsulize their knowledge in a one-day or one-month course, time enough to gain 'spiritual growth', to 'clean the psycho-physical psyche' or to learn '*Sanskrit* without grammar'. The only sign of a special relationship with death is the utter disregard of Varanasi-wallahs for traffic rules. But they certainly have no objection to profiting from the morbid image of their city—almost three-quarters of the population lives off the pilgrim and tourism industry. Life dominates death at all levels.

Thus I prided myself having understood Varanasi when, during an early morning boat ride along the ghats, we rammed into a corpse. The boatman rowed away quickly but for a moment we were confronted with the sight of a bloated, rotting, gone-greenish-blue corpse whose stink lay like a swathe of fog on the water. 'As the ropes soften in the water and finally tear, the corpses float to the surface,' the boatman later explained.

I could not force this memory from my mind. Suddenly I felt the presence of death. At the railway station, I saw how the *bhaddar* agents waylaid the dying and offered to organize their last journey from hospice and temple to the pyre. At the shore of the river, I daily saw thousands shaving their heads after the ritual bath that commemorates the dead. And in the lanes of the old city, warned by the chanted mantra *Ram nam satya hai*, I had time and again to make way for a bier. I was no longer so sure how life and death related to one another in Varanasi.

~

In the kingdom of heat, water is king. Day after day, people drag their emaciated bodies, their fleshy bodies to the river, to reassure themselves of their existence. They step into the water, kneel, pinch their noses and immerse themselves into the river with closed eyes. They feel a freshness on their bodies, they celebrate the blessings they have received, they nurture new desires and hopes. Then they emerge from the water, first their heads, then their torsos, breathe deeply and open their eyes: on the surface of the water floats yellowish foam that stinks worse than a rotting carcass, boils of pus on the holy body. The true believers, a minority like everywhere else, refuse to acknowledge this sacrilege. They love *Ganga* mataji, and their love does not permit them to speak ill of her. 'We will not hear another word,' they retort to the warnings of the environmentalists. 'Be quiet.'

They devote themselves at sunrise to their ritual bath, nothing can restrain them. They would as soon spit into the river as they would spit at their own mother. They do not wash themselves with soap, they do not relieve themselves in the water. But they refuse to accept that the river shows a count of *E. coli* bacillus a thousandfold higher than the permissible levels.

The overwhelming majority, however, pollute the river without a thought and believe that a garland and a coconut settle the balance. The holiness of the river relieves them of personal responsibility. *Ganga*, a goddess after all, should be strong enough to wash away all sins. She needs no protection, no consideration. Dirt only sticks to mortals, the gods are dirt resistant. Hence the people believe they will be cleansed even when *Ganga* is a sewer. The relationship is one-sided. Would it not be better if *Ganga* were a vulnerable child rather than a holy mother?

'Like every believer, I must take my morning bath in *Ganga* mataji,' Veer Bhadra Mishra replied evasively. 'As a scientist I know that I shouldn't even dip my little toe in the river.'

Mahant Mishra, a white-haired gentleman, handsome as an ageing Candide, begins every day with a *snaan* and then attends to his duties as a priest, an engineer and a citizen devoted to the salvation of the *Ganga*. He lives at Tulsi *Ghat* in a house occupied four centuries ago by the people's poet Tulsidas (he is introduced as though he were a neighbour). 'In his day,' said Mahant Mishra, 'the high priests and the Brahmins attacked Tulsidas for sullying the pristine epic with his coarse vernacular, but today everybody swears by his translation of the *Ramayana*.'

At the place where Tulsidas once had a vision of *Hanuman*, there stands today the Sankat Mochan *Mandir*; Veer Bhadra Mishra is the mahant of this temple as the firstborn son in his family has been for generations. He also runs a *Sanskrit* school and a hospice for the dying who are waiting for the salvation promised to all who pass away within the city limits of Varanasi.

'In my youth,' Mahantji recounted, 'people settled down on the ghats and waited for death. There were many simple rooms where one could sleep and do one's cooking. But these days most of the buildings have been put to some other use, and the police do not allow the people to stay at the ghats overnight. I think that there are still many people who come to Varanasi to die, only it is no longer that easy to find a place. Hence we offer a dormitory to poor pilgrims. I don't want to break with this tradition, I come from a very traditional family. Among our forefathers you will find musicians, wrestlers (a well-respected occupation in Varanasi), actors who performed in religious dramas. I was the first one in the family to have been permitted a secular education, and that only because I was rather good at mathematics. My father died early, and I was consecrated as mahant at the age of fourteen. But my mother insisted that I study and complete my schooling. It wasn't always easy. The university did not allow me to attend lectures in my priestly robes, and our tradition forbade me from wearing any other form of clothing. My mother secretly bought me a pair of trousers that I wore when I went to the Banaras Hindu University. I have always felt uncomfortable in them, even later, when as a professor of engineering and hydraulics I had to lecture in one of these colonial safari suits. But I no longer have to waste any thought on this, as I am now retired.'

While we talked, people constantly entered the simple room, touched the feet of Mahantji, who was sitting on a raised, outsize mattress, greeted him, took *darshan* and submitted their requests. The morning is devoted to giving audience. Mahant Mishra, whose warm humour one would like to have as a daily companion, smiles often, with an undercurrent of sternness that hints at a toughness that his kindliness belies.

'We must act soon,' he exclaimed, 'we have lost so much time. In June 1986, the then prime minister, Rajiv Gandhi, inaugurated the Ganges Action Plan at Dasaswamedha *Ghat*, to the fanfare of publicity and with a total budget of over 300 million dollars. Enormous amounts were channelled into monster projects with expensive machinery, and all parties concerned got hefty kickbacks out of it. The interests of heavy industry took charge of all decisions. Medicines were prescribed even before the illness had been properly diagnosed. At one point they even released turtles into the Ganges, around thirty thousand of them, in the hope that they would eat up the corpses. Most of them were poached at once, and the remaining ones seem to have lost their appetite; in any case, today in Varanasi you will not find a single turtle. Not only that, the brass hats neglected to provide for long-term implementation in the Ganges Action Plan budget. Many of the newly constructed plants can no longer be operated for lack of funds. The electric crematorium, which has meanwhile gained social acceptance, is hardly used because of power failures. For five months of the year, during the monsoon, the effluent treatment plants are closed, the pumps do not work, so the waste water is channelled directly into the river. And at the Dasaswamedha *Ghat*, where those politicians assembled at the inauguration on a festooned dais, there burgeons today a huge, open drain from which unfiltered faeces gush into the river.'

Mishra's anger is directed at politicians, bureaucrats and scientists. He counters the cost-intensive inefficiency of all government planning with a vision of his own. Years ago he suggested to the municipal authorities that they build a natural effluent treatment plant that would need no electricity, no chemicals. Developed by an American engineer, this system relies on natural agents of purification such as microbes and algae, the sun and oxygen. In ponds of varying depth, the waste water would be decomposed and purified through fermentation and photosynthesis. The waste water would flow from pond to pond due to gravity. The whole concept is based on nature's self-purifying powers; it takes the holiness of the Ganges in earnest.

'Our recommendation,' Mishra noted wryly, 'has a few grave weaknesses, unfortunately: It is too cheap, it is too easy, it involves the ordinary local people and it could work, and that would put in question all the expensive projects of the government. So it is being contested and undermined all the way by the UP government.'

Which was the first language that *Pandit* Kishan Maharaj, the master of the *tabla*, learnt? When he was born and the midwife brought the baby to the men of the house, the patriarch of the family sang a song in one of his ears and a few bols in the other: *Dha dhin dhin dha / Dha dhin dhin dha / Na tin tin ta / Na dhin dhin dha*. When he turned six, he was initiated as a pupil through a *guru*-shishya ceremony and he

169

begun to practise seriously. *Te re ke ta / te re ke ta.*
Practice was prayer. 'Every session is a yoga of sound,'
says the master, 'through which the musician hopes
to come closer to the pure sound, to dissolve in the
consummate music of the divine.'

Kishan Maharaj never went to school, he studied
with his *guru*, he practised and practised, sometimes
from eight in the evening into the early hours of the
morning when no one could disturb him and he
could focus completely on his instrument. First he
would bathe, then put on a clean, hand-spun cotton
kurta and perform *puja*. Then he would sit down at
the *tabla* and begin to loosen up his fingers with
simple exercises. *Na ge te re / gha re te ge.* The master
found in his own father, Maharaj *Pandit* Kanthe
Maharaj, an exceptional *guru*, respected throughout
India. Father and son took their place in an unbroken
genealogy of masters going back two centuries to the
founder of the Benares gharana, *Pandit Ram* Sahai
Mishra. 'For us he is god,' says the master.

In the alcoves of his spacious practice hall, there
hang life-size portraits of five of his ancestors. On

the opposite wall photographs show the master with *Pandit* Nehru and Indira Gandhi, with Ravi Shankar, and with other acclaimed instrumentalists and vocalists he has accompanied over the years. *Dha dhi na / Na thi na.*

'Only he who has a *guru*,' says the maestro, 'will gain true knowledge.' The *guru* leads you from the darkness of your ignorance to light. He teaches you posture, steadfastness and concentration. He teaches you the correct way of breathing. He demands the utmost perseverance and patience of you. He forces you to play one taal for hours.

Dha - ti re ki ta ta ka / Ta - ti re ki ta ta ka / Thun - ti re ki ta ta ka / Ti - ti re ki ta ta ka.

'Nowadays,' says the master, 'the gurus joke around with their students, they drink with them as if they are friends. In our house there was military discipline.'

After twelve years of instruction, his *guru* explained to him that it is as important to be a good *guru* as it is to be a good musician. 'I only demand of you that you also take a disciple and teach him what

I have taught you,' said the *guru*. 'Do not allow the thread to snap.'

Beside practice and spiritual consciousness, selfless service (sewa) is the third quality that sets a true *guru* apart. In a small *gurukul* next to his house, the master teaches everyone who shows a genuine interest. The students, amongst them an eight-year-old fledgling from the master's family, are playing in synchrony. *Di re di re ki te ta ka / Ti re ti re ki te ta ka.* Shubhshankar, the master's thirteen-year-old nephew, who has already given concerts in Kolkata, Ahmedabad and Ayodhya, joins them and takes the lead role, with a serious expression on his face, back erect, fully aware of the dignity of his position.

'Have you ever felt one with the *tabla*?' I asked *Pandit* Kishan Maharaj as I took my leave. 'Never,' he retorted, annoyed like a *guru* faced with a dull-witted shishya.

~

It's a heavy confusion.
Veda, Koran, holiness, hell, woman, man,
A clay pot shot with air and sperm—

172

When the pot falls apart, what do you call it?
Numbskull! You've missed the point.

One fine morning Pac went alone for a walk along the ghats. Near a black *lingam*, not far from where a few women were wringing out their wet clothes, she saw a man who seemed at first, judging by his slightly bent posture, to be sunk in prayer, but who, she saw from the corner of her eye in passing, was oblivious to the world, lost in masturbation. She hurried on. Shortly afterwards she heard footfalls catching up with her. The man drew alongside, looked at her with expectation and said, in a friendly manner, but with insistence, 'I am also single. Can I come with you?'

Varanasi, the centre of the Hindu cosmos, a place that existed before our current creation and that will survive the next apocalypse, is a paradise of sexual molesters. In the narrow lanes of the city, all fair-skinned breasts and backsides are grabbed and pinched, regardless of whether the tourists are clad in a modest salwar-*kurta* or in provocatively

173

casual beachwear. The outrage of the victim is met with laughter.

In the evenings, the young women in our guesthouse who were travelling on their own exchanged their daily quota of humiliations. The stories were not new to me, they similarly took place in Mumbai. During *Ganesh* Chaturthi, when hundreds of thousands throng the Chowpatty beach, I repeatedly had to threaten loitering men of innocent mien with a beating because they had groped my companion. The importunity of men in India, as foreign and Indian women confirm unanimously, is vulgar and insulting.

Within the family, the woman, in the person of one's own mother, is usually held in high esteem. Women outside the fold of the family, however, are not accorded the same respect. The sexual is dragged into the open because it is repressed or cornered in the private sphere. Within the four walls of one's home, one must conform to numerous traditions, codes of conduct and expectations, but once out of the door one can let oneself go. A high degree of sexual frustration limits the behaviour towards women to lewd passes. The holy mother, be it one's own or *Ganga* mataji, and the victims of one's lust and covetousness, be they unaccompanied women or unprotected rivers, belong to two different worlds. One's own sister is not allowed into the street unaccompanied, and if she must go out, she has to be modestly veiled, but the sisters of other young men are fair game.

This schizophrenia also extends into the idealized precincts of belief, which are protected by fanatical consistency. The followers of *Hindutva*, the self-proclaimed, radical defenders of Hinduism, for example, do nothing to safeguard the Ganges, but they forcibly prevent the well-known director Deepa Mehta from shooting a film about the fate of Varanasi's abandoned widows, on the grounds that it would besmirch the holy city's reputation. Ideals and personal conduct, the private sphere and public space, rhetoric and reality come apart, with horrifying consequences.

Mother, I've poured glory on both families!
I ate twelve husbands at my father's house
and sixteen at the in-laws.

I tied sister-in-law and mother-in-law
to the bed, and insulted
brother-in-law.
I burned the part of the hair of that hag
who nagged me.
In my womb I got five
plus two plus four.
I ate the neighbour lady for breakfast
along with the wise old mother.
Poor thing! Then spreading the easy bed,
I stretched my legs and slept.
Now I don't come, don't go,
don't die or live.
The master has erased all shame.
Seizing the name, I dropped the world.
I caught the name—
So near!
I saw the name!
shouts Kabir.

~

The poet yearns passionately to capture *Ganga*'s flow in words. His strophes have barely found a form when the river, this raga of flow and undertow, changes its course, and he has to sing it again. But this hymn, too, is washed away soon after; *Ganga* has once again changed the course that he had to depict. The poet was caught up in a whirlpool of devotion. But perhaps *Ganga* would respond, perhaps she would climb the *ghat*, each step a frame, a poem, a prayer, until she laps around the poet, embraces and liberates him.

Exit Darkness

Patna's main railway station was brightly lit, the information panels glowing pale blue as if they wanted to outshine all the dim prejudices about Bihar. But when we stepped out of the building, we sank into a deep darkness, from which the rough voices of rickshaw-wallahs emerged. Headlamps curved round the circular traffic in front of the railway station; everything else was left to one's overwhelmed fantasy. The city was struck with blindness and stank of exhaust fumes. The rickshaw-wallahs hastened behind their voices, hope igniting in their numerous faces like a poorly lit match. Because of our luggage we had to take two rickshaws, and they slid into even deeper darkness the moment we left the roundabout behind us. There were no streetlights, not a window glowed.

When a car approached us, I could see the silhouette of the man pedalling strenuously in front of me, and when a vehicle overtook us I could see his shredded undershirt held together by a few tenacious threads. A few normal signs of habitation—drunken laughter, dry barking—increased the feeling of menace that emanated from this city of powerless millions. At the end of the broad road along which we jerked and jolted, something shimmered. It turned out to be a hotel with a generator. Even the driveway was well lit. In Patna evidently only places of transit were illuminated.

The rickshaw-wallah, giving us a guided tour of Patna's colonial quarter the next day, spilt his sorrows at every traffic light—during the day they actually worked. He never left his daughter alone at home, neither during the day nor at night. He would bring her to school in the morning and fetch her himself in the afternoon. If she wanted to meet her friends, she could do that at home. 'But surely kidnapping only affects the rich of the city,' I asked.

'Not at all,' he said and turned around to look at us while going at full speed. 'Everyone is in danger!

Only last month the daughter of a colleague was kidnapped, and since then there has been no news of her.'

~

Patna's main landmark is a colossal monument to
failure: a seemingly futuristic, conical granary that
was constructed after the dreadful famine of 1770 by
a British officer named John Garstin, whose initial
plan had been to gradually fill the silo through an
opening at its top. But despite the best intentions,
the granary had not prevented a single famine in the
two hundred years that have passed. Not because of
the doors that swing inwards and thus cannot be
opened when the warehouse is full, and not because
of the steps on both sides that are too steep for load-
bearing coolies, as legends like to claim. The truth is
that nobody knows why the Golghar has never been
filled. From the time of its completion, visitors have
had ample opportunity to marvel at the wonderful
echo in the empty silo.

From a distance, the structure—it could hold
137,000 tons of grain or rice—resembles an atomic
reactor; stepping closer one can decipher the confident

inscription, 'For the perpetual relief of famine', inscribed in the languages of administrative glory, English and Persian. At least its adjacent grounds were being used. The lawns were covered with saris spread out to dry; from the viewers' gallery, they looked like the colourful rings of a planet. Not far away flowed the *Ganga*, several kilometres wide, unploughed by boat keels. At the Buddha *ghat*, wood was piled up for salvation—bamboo for the bier, *bulgingu* trunks for the pyre. And on the quay wall was written in scrawny letters: ROTI, KAPDA AUR MAKAN. From the top of an empty silo, one can survey the whole of creation.

The other landmark, an Islamic library, where some of the last remaining manuscripts from the Al-Andalusian University of Cordoba are kept, was unfortunately closed; the third landmark stretched over the Ganges, a long bridge over a river that has always lacked bridges: the last one was more than a hundred kilometres behind us, the next one would follow a week's journey downstream. We stopped our rickshaw, like many other rickshaws and cars, in

184

the middle of the bridge, got off, looked down in to the water and silently mouthed a wish. Such a wish, our driver assured us, is always fulfilled.

Opposite the maidan, a slushy field that attracted garbage and pigs, the cinema halls of the city stood one next to the other. The rickshaw-wallah convinced us that it was too risky to look in for the night show at nine o'clock; so we approached the counter shortly before dusk, only to hear that *Nayak*, the current show, was sold out. Next to the ticket counter was a kiosk for snacks and drinks. A man beckoned us to come closer. 'Do you want to see the film?'

'Yes.'

'Give me Rs 100.'

He fished a wad of tickets out of his shirt pocket, the crumpled explanation for the sold-out show, and peeled off two tickets. We hesitated; the regular price of the most expensive tickets was only Rs 20. The man indicated that he could make the tickets disappear just as quickly and miraculously as they had appeared if we did not pay the demanded price. Behind us, a multitude of eager young men, queuing up for the cheap seats, stared at us without batting an eyelid or making a comment. A feeling of shame spread from my back across the whole of my body. Despite this I handed over a hundred-rupee note surreptitiously. The man unfolded it and held it against the light for all to see. We pocketed the tickets and withdrew into an inconspicuous corner of the yard, where we were soon accosted by the bravest amongst the inquisitive.

A little while later, a man appeared at the top of the outer staircase and invited us to enter the cinema building, although general entry had not been announced yet. Four men were sitting next to a locked icebox in the plush interior. It was stiflingly hot in the room, but the men did not have the key to the cold drinks. Apart from us, a gentleman accompanied by two women in heavy make-up and three stylishly dressed young men had been allowed in. Their shirts bulged with prosperity. We wondered why the six o'clock show had not yet begun although it was getting on for seven. 'In Bihar,' one of the three young men said, 'everything starts late, even the films. What do you expect? We are in Lalooland. Do you know who Laloo is? In the old days, Bihar was the most civilized region of our country, the heart of *Bharat*. A centre of science and culture. Then came Laloo *Prasad* Yadav. The erstwhile chief minister and the husband of the current chief minister has pushed Bihar into an abyss,' the three men explained to us in good English. 'But we vote for the *BJP*,' their spokesman stood up as if emphasize his words, 'we are *RSS* soldiers.'

'Oh,' I said, 'you are involved in *mara-mari?*'

'No! No!' Laughter.

'I see, you are soldiers of the mind?'

Nodding heads and even more laughter.

'We are fighting for a clean and honest Bihar.'

'How come then you have been allowed in here before all the others?'

The three men smiled indulgently; we wouldn't be able to understand the explanation, their silence conveyed. The spokesman, a handsome man with a cultivated moustache and well-styled hair, was the head of a small pharmaceutical company, a rather difficult task in Lalooland, if one was to believe his stories told with an insistent smirk on his face. He introduced himself as Rajan and hastily added that the name was derived from the *Sanskrit* word for king. 'King Mahendra,' his two friends shouted with well-rehearsed laughter, pointing at him. 'That's what we call him: King Mahendra.'

'Who was King Mahendra?' I asked.

A powerful landlord who, like Rajan, was involved in the pharmaceutical business, and who, unlike their friend, had made a fortune. When he entered politics, he introduced a new election campaign style: he had his opponents killed. And whoever threatened to vote for an opponent was bought, beaten or shot. He had retained his seat in the state assembly in every election since 1980, first as a member of the Congress party and later as an MLA of Laloo Yadav's Rashtriya Janata Dal (*RJD*).

The laughter increased. With these young men every comment on the present turned into a cynical joke. However, the spokesman turned serious when he started explaining that the name of the film's main actress—Rani Mukherjee—was also of *Sanskrit* origin and meant queen. 'A beautiful name,' he said, with solemn voice and glowing eyes, as if it were the name of a rare jewel. He did not mention Rani Mukherjee's beautiful round face or her erotic radiance, he simply transfigured her into an icon because of her name. In the course of our conversation, it became clear that Rajan only found happiness in the present when he could relate it to the past, to the supposedly golden age of Hinduism. His knowledge of *Sanskrit*, a vague residue from his schooldays, was the connection to this lost paradise.

The main character of *Nayak*—that means hero or supreme commander in *Sanskrit*, Rajan had explained—turned out to be a contemporary *Arjuna* in the *avatar* of a TV reporter who blows away the evils of corruption, injustice and despotism like a whirlwind. He was played by a somewhat ageing Anil Kapoor (Anil, not to forget, owes its existence to the *Sanskrit* word for air). When he challenges the chief minister in a live interview, he is asked to take up his position for a single day so that he would get to know the burden of the office. But instead of backing out, Anil tidies up Maharashtra in a jiffy and wins a landslide victory in the next election. Even the King Mahendra-like methods of his enemies—he loses his parents in a bomb blast directed against him—cannot deter him from his righteous crusade. He is rewarded with the heart of Rani, a natural and pure beauty from the village. In the end, he resurrects a second Singapore out of the slums of Mumbai. His fight is directed against all the corrupt and oppressive institutions, especially the police, who are portrayed as being completely hand in glove with the cynical elite in power. (A few days after we left Patna, four people were killed and hundreds injured when the police opened fire on a demonstration against the massive increase in unsolved kidnappings and murders.) In a memorable scene, one of the characters complained that the situation had become just as bad as in Bihar; the audience burst out in loud and persistent laughter and then applauded wildly, full of a local patriotism that was proud to be acknowledged, in whatever way, by a technically brilliant production from Bombay. I would have loved to hear how Rajan had liked this fairy-tale story with a future-oriented twist, but like the rest of the audience he had rushed off into Lalooland as soon the credits began to roll.

Professor Sinha and the Susas

Professor Sinha, born sixty kilometres south of the Ganges, encountered the river for the first time when his grandmother was cremated. During the ceremony he saw several dolphins. He wondered why they kept coming out of the water. Years later he registered at Patna University to study zoology and spent every free minute on the banks watching the dolphins. Whenever he crossed the Ganges, they playfully accompanied the ferry. It fascinated him that the mammals loved to be near human beings. Even in November, when the Chhat festival is celebrated in Patna and more than a million people gather on the banks of the river, he could spot the dolphins from the ghats. As a young lecturer in Monghyr, he would walk every evening to the promenade to watch them in the light of the setting sun. His curiosity grew over time, and the questions that arose in his mind were not answered by the existing scientific literature. He started dissecting stranded dolphins. When the Ganges Action Plan was passed, he suddenly had funds to devote himself to the research work he had dreamed of carrying out for years. Professor Sinha became the world's leading specialist in the *Platanista gangetica*. His undiminished fascination for the dolphin stems from the fact that some of its mysteries are still unresolved. It is well-known that this dolphin, two and a half metres long and weighing almost a hundred kilos, can vaguely distinguish between darkness and light and never eats dead fish. But how does it distinguish between living and dead fish? It is also known that it swims on one side and drags the other fin over the slimy river bed, thus orienting itself in the changing currents of the Ganges and moving about even in water that is only thirty centimetres deep. But the functioning of its sonar orientation system has remained a secret.

In a Patna of ubiquitous garbage, the university campus seemed like an oasis despite its evident disrepair, and Professor Sinha's laboratory, equipped with an air-conditioner and an arsenal of internationally competitive computers and printers, was its spring. The corridor was lined with photographs of dolphins emerging from the water and happily smiling students in small motorboats. Ever since Professor Sinha dedicated himself to the research into dolphins, their number in the Ganges has remained fairly constant at 1,500.

'The Yadavs, the milkmen,' the professor explained in a voice that did not seem to allow much excitement, 'viewed the dolphin as a river cow and therefore did not allow it to be killed.' That gave us the idea of referring to the dolphin as the holy cow of the holy Ganges. We even thought up a small song:

Susa iski gai hai! Ganga hamari mai hai!
Susa iska phul hai! Isko marna bhul hai!

The dolphin is *Ganga*'s cow, *Ganga* is our mother!
The dolphin is *Ganga*'s bloom, don't kill it, you won't find another!

'Thus we underline a traditional cultural taboo. The dolphins are killed because half of their body consists of fat from which oil is extracted—for medicinal use, as bait and for massage. It's a recent phenomenon that poor people have started eating its meat, which used to be taboo for all except a certain sub-caste of fishermen. But today mutton is expensive and the most important edible fish, the large Indian carp, widely and inexpensively available twenty years ago, has become a speciality. Yields in Bihar have reduced by more than half in the last three decades. Today fishing is completely under the control of a mafia of rich entrepreneurs, who are connected with the authorities and the police. They are the modern successors of the feudal lords who until recently owned the river with all the fish in it. These entrepreneurs lease a stretch of the river from the government and extract even the smallest fish using huge, extremely fine-meshed nets. Traditional fishermen who protest against such practices are manhandled by their goons. Sometimes these entrepreneurs poison a part of the river and kill all marine life in a stretch of several kilometres. Or they use dynamite. On the whole, the number of animals has not reduced; however, the quantity of economically utilizable fish stock has fallen drastically. Surprisingly, even today, the Ganges supplies almost 90 per cent of the Indian spawn. In fact, there is a direct train link between Patna and Calcutta exclusively for the purpose of transporting spawn.'

After we had given Professor Sinha an exact description of the place where we had encountered the dolphins, he told us about the regular field research he carries out with students on the lower part of the Ganges. 'Four times river pirates have attacked us. Once, just as we had made a landfall near Sultanganj, we were suddenly surrounded by heavily armed men. They ordered us to stand in a line, as if staging an execution. They pointed their AK-47s at us and threatened to shoot us. I held a GPS in my right hand, a reference book on birds in my left hand, a pair of binoculars around my neck. "If you tell us who you are, we might spare your lives," one of the river pirates said.

"'I am a teacher, and these are my students.'

"'Why the binoculars?'

"'To observe birds.'

"'Can't you observe them without this thing?'

"'Not clearly enough to be able to compare them with the pictures in my book. When I get too close to them, they fly away.'

"'Well, your explanations are not devoid of a certain logic,' he said after pondering for a while.

'His choice of words made it clear to me that he was well educated and I asked him who he was.

"'I am the leader of this group. We are all Yadavs fighting against the fishermen. We camp on sandbanks such as these and attack boats like yours because they usually transport weapons. But your boat contains only books. We were mistaken, you can go now.'"

Ahimsa and terror

Bihar is a state plagued by flood and drought, by a violence of giving and taking. Death was present in all the eyewitness accounts I had read in preparation. But the violence was not visible in the landscape.

Flat earth, sated rice fields, rows of trees on embankments, low hillocks in the background. Sometimes palm trees. Like Bali without terraces. Cakes of cow dung were plastered on the walls of houses, on the sides of bridges, on road signs—ornaments of survival. Pilgrims crouched on the rooftops of buses, wrapped in colourful cloth of the cheapest material. It was that time of year when one commemorated one's dead ancestors. The road—built with Japanese funding so that Buddhist visitors could reach Bodh Gaya on a 'highway'—was full of holes. It took us three hours to cover the ninety kilometres. We drove through Jehanabad, a district in which thousands of people have been massacred in the past two decades. A kind of low-intensity civil war rages between landlords and the landless, a continuation of the daily terror of indentured labour (for two kilos of rice per day), hunger and degradation by other means. The Yadavs had transformed themselves into a class of the newly rich and powerful that—depending on the occasion—either fought against the old establishment or supported it and its death squadrons, the Ranvir Sena.

Parties like the *RJD* that had been formed to represent the interests of the weaker and deprived sections of society were now protecting the interests of an upstart elite. The split between the privileged and the unprivileged went right through the lower, the so-called backward, castes.

Due to a puncture shortly after Jehanabad, we were delayed beyond nightfall. We were increasingly nervous. The hotel in Patna had warned us against travelling after sunset, and our driver proved to be night-blind. At every pair of headlights hurtling towards us, he braked almost to a halt and veered to the edge of the road and nearly into the gutter.

The exhausted driver stopped for *chai* in a village with a single row of shops that owed its existence to the highway. A bunch of people stared at a small TV set through the unglazed windows of a tea shop. Next to the TV, a cook hunkered down on his heels and prepared rotis on an open fire. The rotis were accompanied by a vegetable mash slapped on a tin plate. The guests ate quietly and mechanically. The walls were unadorned. On the TV screen one could see a black cloud over a Manhattan skyline, a clumsy scene from one of those third-rate films that are produced direct to video. A draught blew the smoke from the open fire across the TV screen and veiled the view. When the smoke had passed, a newsreader occupied the screen. The volume was not loud enough for me to understand. I only heard her mentioning the Pentagon. The growing mass of human beings moved in closer. The screen showed a crumbled building, the subtitle claimed it was the Pentagon. An aeroplane had crashed into the Pentagon? I looked around, the faces showed no expression. The man to my left had a wound on his neck that was partly scabbed and partly suppurating, with a few flies resting on it. The cook began to scold the waiter; he wiped his hands angrily on a dirty towel. The voice of the newsreader was drowned out by a truck engine. The screen showed smoke billowing out of the skyscrapers. Somebody tugged at my shirt. Behind me was a woman—with one hand she continued to tug at my shirt and with the other she gesticulated jerkily towards her mouth, the fingers tightly closed.

People continued to stare at me expressionlessly. I turned away and hurried back to our taxi. A slightly better dressed man was standing next to it; he asked me in broken English whether the Third World War would break out. He gave us the news. 'These people here,' he explained with spent insight, 'will never understand what has happened. You know, sir, one does not get used to terror. One cannot sleep at night for fear that the house might be burned down, that someone could come to kill you. It never ends, and we don't get used to it. Nobody in our country cares about the terror here. When there is a strike, dozens of workers are gunned down. When there is a flood, thousands are drowned. But we are not important, we are not in New York, that will lead to the Third World War, no?'

I tried to rid him of this worry, but he shook off my arguments.

'It is nice,' he said abruptly, 'that tourists like you come to Bihar. Do you know the origin of the name Jehanabad? It's a Persian word, it means "the city of the world".'

~

Where Gautama once attained enlightenment, one can today admire a brightly polished pedestrian street that seems to suggest that Buddhism brings about prosperity and demands a higher level of cleanliness and order. The sanctuary was shrouded in silence; the pilgrims sauntered with slow steps around the Bodhi that once gave shade to enlightenment. During the Buddha's lifetime, this tree supposedly reached a height of almost a hundred metres, but then it was pruned by several hostile rulers and eventually felled. It has recovered only because it was granted exile in the Sri Lankan city of Anuradhapura and from there—centuries later—resettled at home. Underneath this tree, thus it is said, the Buddha gained the enlightenment that there is no need for god, that the deed is more decisive than the soul, that idols should not be worshipped.

In the Mahabodhi temple, a devotee stretched out on the floor worked on the feet of the golden Buddha with smacking devotion.

Bihar—the name itself derived from vihara, a Buddhist monastery—was the scene of early

Buddhism: the land of Gautama's Enlightenment, of his early ascetic disciples, of his first monasteries and of the most impressive university ever run in his name. But Buddhism was driven out of Bihar and the place called Bodh Gaya sank into oblivion until it was rediscovered in 1877. Since the 1930s, when the Mahabodhi temple was handed back to the Buddhists, the active construction of temples and monasteries has converted this village at the end of the world into a cosmopolitan monument. Tibet and Burma built two impressive monasteries. Thailand contributed a Wat temple. Japan financed two temples and a nearly thirty-metre-high Buddha statue. China, Vietnam, Sri Lanka and Bhutan erected prayer halls in their respective national styles. In 1992 Nepal inaugurated the Temang monastery and even Laos has built a sacred embassy. Other projects are planned: a gigantic Maitreya statue, the future incarnation of the Enlightened One, which is expected to overshadow all previous Buddhas. The laying of the foundation was, however, delayed when news of an even bigger statue arrived from China. What followed was an architectural contest over the world's largest tribute to the Compassionate, the Blessed, the Wise and the Understanding One.

We would have remembered our days in Bodh Gaya as a sleepy, somewhat unreal intermezzo in our journey through Bihar but for the appearance of Vishwakarma, a man with wings and four arms whose hands hold an axe, a hammer, a bow and a set of scales. And, as one might expect from the god of crafts, he crushed, hammered and dissected the silence of Bodh Gaya into sounds that wouldn't have emanated even from *Shiva*'s *damru*. In a pandal opposite our hotel, a few solitary devotees were witnesses to this spectacle. The papier-mâché figure of the Architect of the Universe, who formed heaven and earth and gave names to the gods, was surrounded by screaming lights and glittering pop music, like a Las Vegas illusionist. However, there was no tense expectation to be felt. A few men sat on plastic chairs, unsusceptible to the destruction of the world. A few passers-by took *darshan* and a few grains of *prasad* and continued on their way. When the sound waves subsided, Bodh Gaya regained the silence of a spiritual spa. Not even the rattling of a rickshaw could be heard in the pedestrian street. Dark-skinned women swept the floor, Japanese groups allowed the cameras to choreograph their pilgrimage. The sweepers and the tourists glided on the asphalted peace like flies.

~

In the sixth century BC, the principle of Ahimsa was developed in the area that is today Bihar. The concept of radical non-violence was formulated and put into practice by the parishads, communities of hermits living in the forests that in those days covered most of the land. This magnetic field also influenced Jainism and Advaita. In all three religious concepts, non-violence is defined far more extensively than the usual understanding of not harming other creatures. According to Advaita you practise violence when you term the other as 'other'. The concept of atman, the omnipresent soul, sees every human being as infinite and unlimited, and therefore he is not equal to his neighbours but merged with them as well as with god. If one limits one's neighbour, one limits oneself. Ahimsa opposes any language of segregation, it calls upon us always to see the common behind the divisive. As a result, Ahimsa could protect humans against manipulation through fictive identities, whether of a national, ethnic or cultural character.

But in Bihar people are murdered every day because they are different. In the whole of India, which is increasingly becoming like Bihar, this loss of one's own spiritual roots, this debunking of one's own philosophical tradition, is accepted without protest. The daily terror is noted and commented on, but without objection, without resistance. The worst thing about social inequality, the caste system and the feudal structure, is the erosion of the core of humanity: not to accept wrong. Injustice and violence have become a fixture of life. With the ethics of Advaita and Ahimsa, Indian religion reaches its highest pinnacle and suffers its worst failure at the same time. Deeply rooted injustice and incessantly invented differences lead ethics into an absurd impasse, driving it out of the areas of practised morality into the spheres of abstract thinking—as beautiful and yet as unreachable as a celestial body.

The stranded steamer, the silent anchorite and the end of the handkerchief killers

At the Lal Darwaza *Ghat* in Monghyr, an old paddle-steamer, the *MS Benares*, lay on the shore, rusty, the deck broken, the yellow and black chimney slanted like those of sinking ships in the children's books of old. A few Jugendstil windows leaned against the light, two deck chairs were well placed for an amorous couple to enjoy. But the paint must have worn down overnight. The captain's cabin was occupied: sandals, clothes on a chair, a mosquito net hung up. In the control room somebody had set up a simple workshop. The wreck now belonged to a local company. I was explicitly warned by several passers-by against 'trespassing' (another one of these vitally important English words that have crept into the languages of India) when I tried to climb on to the deck via the anchorage. A young boy rode by on a buffalo, a few workers shovelled sand on to a truck. The boy and the workers laughed together about a sketch that was being transmitted on radio. A corpse wrapped in orange cloth was carried on a bier to the river. The boy stopped in front of a reed hut, the workers wiped the sweat off their foreheads with the backs of their hands, the procession laid the bier on the funeral pyre. Two *paan*-wallahs waited for the next ritual. I stretched myself out on one of the deck chairs and spent some time observing a munching cow in front of a full trough, ruminating on dreams of trade, prosperity and happiness on the Ganges. Of merchants in the centuries before our time who were the first to commercially utilize the waterway. There were seaports in the middle of India, and goods were distributed all the way to China and East Africa. Later, the fleets of the Gosain sadhus dominated trade on the Ganges. The network of sadhus, a result of their innumerable pilgrimages, was the basis of a wide-ranging commercial empire. And as the sadhus normally travelled in large, armed groups, their goods were well protected. The situation changed when the East India Company decided to introduce a regular ship service. In 1828 a paddle-wheel steamer left Calcutta for Allahabad. Ten days later, the steamer sailed past Monghyr; after twenty-three days it reached Allahabad, a distance that would have taken three months by road. Encouraged by this success, the Company had three low-draught steel ships manufactured: they were shipped to Calcutta and assembled there. In the autumn of 1834, the first of these steamed away for Allahabad. The journey was as dangerous as shifting river banks and pirates. Insurance companies in Calcutta charged the same premium as for the fifteen-thousand-kilometre-long journey to England. And the berths cost as much as the passage from London to New York. But the introduction of the railways dealt the death blow to the era of steamers, and in a town like Monghyr it was now impossible to find even a single boat that could have taken us a little way further down the Ganges.

After we had chugged with a rickshaw from *ghat* to *ghat* and had insistently inquired with every ferryman, fisherman, washerman and bather, we happened upon a man who claimed to be in a position to help us. He sat on a railing, one leg dangling, the other holding the balance; he was dressed in a safari suit, the one-time preferred uniform of the local representatives of the British Empire. He did not disclose which office or company he worked for, but he knew all the places downriver and the distance to them. First he pronounced in profuse words the hopelessness of our wish, supported by the sight of a wrecked ship behind him. Then he gave us a ray of hope and tagged a price on to it. We did not know which or whose boat he was offering us, or whether it was legal, but in any case we were unable to pay the exorbitant price he demanded. The man did not seem to regret our refusal. He was unwilling to bargain, he dismissed us with a flick of the hand, as though we were petitioners whose audience had come to an end.

It was the morning after the end of a fair. There was a lot of wiping and sweeping, the flowers were thrown on to garbage heaps, where they immediately became garbage, the remaining items of ritual were

209

packed, the contented traders chatted and smoked their first relaxed cigarette after a month of keen business. Sultanganj was undergoing a major clean-up after the pilgrimage month of Srawan, *Shiva*'s month, during which hundreds of thousands of people had visited the temple on the rocky island near the *ghat*. Loaded with a pot of *Gangajal*, they had set off barefoot to Deogarh, more than a hundred kilometres away, where they had poured the *Ganga* water on the *lingam* of a local *Shiva* temple. A foot march of three days, but one that the fastest of pilgrims covered in twenty hours, as a wiry trader assured me; he himself covers the distance at a running pace, halting every two hours for a brief rest.

A few boulders lay in front of the *ghat*, like bales that had fallen from a ship damaged at sea. Relief sculptures had been chiselled into the stone, amongst them *Ganga* in a reclining posture, lascivious and a little over-weight but stretched out splendidly like an ageing Bollywood diva. Above her navel, 'Eveready' promised eternal battery power in garish red.

The temple on the island, with its multitude of doors and gates and towers, was reminiscent of a medieval fortress. The water level was so low that one could not reach the temple by boat; one had to trudge through a knee-deep mire. A *pujari* appeared from behind a balustrade and guided me with gestures through the mire. I waded into the safe harbour of the temple. After washing my feet in a small basin, I climbed on to a platform cemented around a willow, the bark as old as the gods and painted in the orange of worship. A voice commanded me to climb up a steep staircase with as many twists and turns as the Upanishads. The staircase opened onto bare, empty cells, made of brick, on both sides. The stairs finally led to the sanctum sanctorum where three lingams and stones decorated with flowers uplifted the general pallor. Everything else was left to prayer. Two pujaris appeared and blessed me heavy-handedly. They accepted my offering with as much interest as an overfed person does another sweet. They asked me whether I wanted to pay Babaji a visit. I agreed, and they led me over several levels and turnings to a cosily furnished room. The fairly young and smug *Baba* sat on a mattress. He did not respond to my greeting. He did not say anything. I smiled politely and mentioned our *Ganga* journey. He smiled back politely. I couldn't think of anything that I could ask the holy man. The way he sat before me, in a posture of complete balance and seemingly at peace with himself, his smile invited me to stay at this place for a while, tired as I was after months of travelling. And he certainly would have understood had I just sat there for a few days and shared with him this room outside of time. But my good upbringing, often an annoying companion, urged me to seek conversation, compelled me to ask one of these dim-witted questions—Where from? Where to?—to which I myself often fall victim. Babaji picked up a small board from the floor, which I had not noticed until then, and with the first word that he wrote with a piece of chalk, I realized he must have taken an oath of silence. Now scores of questions occurred to me, questions that he answered briefly, sometimes in English, sometimes in Hindi, writing slowly like a first grader. He had been living in this temple for thirteen years; he had not spoken for thirteen years. He would remain silent forever. But that did not mean that there were no limits to his sacrifice. On one of the walls hung a sizeable collection of photographs that showed Babaji in front of temples and at festivals, or amidst the masses at the Kumbh Mela. How surprising that we did not see one another there, I joked; he smiled back with equanimity, as he had at each of my questions. He only asked me why we were on a *Ganga yatra*, and he smiled at my answer. I asked him why he had taken an oath of silence, and he smiled in reply without writing anything on his small board. Instead he gave me two handfuls of *prasad* that made my trouser pockets bulge. The pujaris accompanied me on the way out, they wished to take a bath in the glowing red sunset.

On the way from the *ghat* to the bazaar, we were joined by a growing number of boys. I distributed the *prasad* from the temple, the boys thanked us politely. Once we reached the bazaar, our spontaneous procession blocked the traffic. In the hope of shaking off our followers, I opted for a shave in a barber's salon that was just wide enough for the barber to stand comfortably behind his customer's chair. In the mirror I saw the faces of countless children gawking at me. The barber's colleague became a show-master who deftly answered all the questions about who—what—where as if he was well acquainted with my biography. I stretched my left hand out and asked the public for an entrance fee. The joke back-fired on me, the shaving blade jerked dangerously. The traffic on the main road broke down completely when a bus stopped in front of the salon because the driver, as well as all his passengers, did not want to miss the spectacle of my evening shave. The unrestrained honking only disturbed those who were honking. The barber was in no hurry either, he savoured the great moment. When checking on his work, he felt several bristly places on my neck that he touched up with great devotion, while outside the gaping, honking and screaming continued—all the energy of Sultanganj seemed to be concentrated in front of the salon. The barber massaged my cheeks and my chin; he sprayed water on my face and wiped it off carefully; he

214

rubbed cream on to my face and combed my hair. He applied all the measures that he had learnt in a long professional life and finally demanded a very modest fee for his services. I stepped out of the door, where my faithful following received me—only the bus driver had not awaited the end of my shave.

~

Geographical terms are a cause of eternal misunder-standings. Had Columbus continued his foot march for another ten days, he would have probably reached the Orinoco, named it the Ganges, and no one would take offence today. Similarly, only those travellers equipped with old reports, exact maps and a lot of time would notice that a British officer did not understand the name Kahalgaon properly or perhaps intentionally distorted it, and thus the town opposite two beautiful islands was called Colganj and sometimes even Colgong.

Lunch was sacred to the boatmen, but they will-ingly shared it with us. We ordered a round of *chai* and a few chapattis. It was impossible, one of the boatmen said, to go down the Ganges on a small boat in this season because no one could row upstream against the strong current on the return journey. We had just reconciled ourselves to the thought of further journeys in overcrowded trains when a smartly dressed man approached us. He spoke a slow, but correct, English. And he infused each of his statements with a high degree of authority. The sadness that surrounded him, as well as his crippled foot, further distinguished him from other men. He confirmed that it would be impossible to travel down the river in a boat but suggested that we hire a boat to the two islands nearby. We could leave our luggage with him, for he was the manager of the coal warehouse behind us. We laid our backpacks on a bench. The other half of the room was occupied by a large table. 'You can trust me,' he said, 'I have served a long tenure in the army.'

'Kargil?' I asked.

He nodded. 'My injury was no coincidence. I had killed too much. In the end I didn't even know how many I had killed. I did not want to return home. I was offered a job in this warehouse. I fulfil my duties conscientiously. You need not worry. I don't know if you will find the temples on the islands interesting. Actually there is no reason to come here. Don't pay more than Rs 50 for the boat. I shall wait for you here.'

There was an *ashram* on each of the islands, but we could not visit the first one because of a spiteful *sadhu* who did not allow us to land. There were no sadhus to be seen on the second island. The walls of the Tapas *Ashram* were covered with holy portraits of many beliefs: the Buddha, Mahavir, Mirabai, Kabir, Vivekananda, Jesus, Guru Tegh Bahadur, Sai Baba, Sri Ramana Maharishi. The painter had signed his work with a childlike signature, and he had left his telephone number and address next to one of the saints, in case another ecumenically inclined client should stray to this place. One of these two densely forested islands with sinless white buildings had supposedly housed the headquarters of the Thugs in their heyday. At the beginning of the nineteenth century, the East India Company, worried about its monopoly on robbery and provoked by attacks of the Thugs on sepoys, commissioned a major general by the name of William Sleeman to

finish them off. It took him two decades to achieve
this, twenty years of fastidious espionage, solid torture
and unrelenting search for potential traitors. A
difficult venture, for the Thugs were more than just
a group of highway robbers. They defined themselves
as a secret society, a guild and a religious community
(their recruits were both Hindus and Muslims!) that
lived according to strict and ancient norms—they
appear in literature for the first time in the year
1356. The booty was a worldly fringe benefit; above
all theirs was a holistic concept of life. The norms of
the Thugs pertained to ritual, but also dealt with
most practical questions; they defined the initiation
ceremony (an oath on the goddess Bhawani with
raised axe) as well as the execution of the raids. After
the victims had been strangled with a knotted handkerchief, they would be beheaded and the bodies and
the heads would be buried in different places so that
they would not be found and identified. These secret
burial spots were located along the main traffic
routes in northern India, at regular intervals—like
motels. The Thugs were strict adherents to their

strategies of robbery. They prepared their attacks carefully and over long periods of time. They sent some of their own ahead, disguised as holy men or respected traders, to gain the confidence of other travellers and to join their caravans. The Thugs were masters of disguise and playacting.

Most probably it was the lax handling of one of their laws that helped the stubborn British officer to capture two dozen high-ranking Thugs and force them to talk. Each one of them, accountants of death, had painstakingly recorded their victims throughout their careers of crime. Ramzan, for example, had added up 604 murders, Burhan had strangled 931 travellers. The secrets of the Thugs were unravelled in a British court by a pale judge, whose wig caused him great discomfort in the stifling heat. A banal, inglorious end to a unique secret society.

The second island only had disappointments to offer, and we soon returned. The backpacks still lay on the bench, but the veteran had disappeared.

A sovereign day

I don't know how we managed to get on to the train from Kahalgaon to Sahibganj. When it arrived at the station, it was already brimming over, and there were hundreds of passengers waiting on the platform. Cycles and milk cans were tied firmly to the window grills, sacks with chillies, firewood or other heavy loads blocked the passages. Two women heaved a huge basket up and pressed it into the mass of passengers. The newspaper on the basket fluttered to reveal stacks of cowdung cakes that were to be sold in the next town for Rs 4 a piece. One of the women just about managed to hang onto the door, alongside two latecomers. They were joined by adventurous boys who tested their courage by surfing the headwind with their bodies. On the roof travelled those who could not afford a ticket and who did not want a confrontation with the ticket inspector. On appearing, he withdrew in a flurry when a woman whose ticket he wanted to see replied with a volley of shouts. 'He is afraid,' the man standing next to me remarked.

A young man squeezed his way through the central passage, holding two plastic bags full of plants with roots, which he tenderly protected. He stopped next to us, placed the plastic bags carefully between his legs, evidently settling down to a long conversation. 'My name is Paras. I am also going to Sahibganj.'

Paras lived with the family that his eldest sister had married into. He had recently finished college and was searching for a suitable university. He started telling us of the many beautiful sights of Sahibganj and of the mission school he had attended. He invited us—for eating, washing, sleeping—to a regal dwelling, as we were to find out soon, a two-storeyed, more than hundred-year-old building. A narrow veranda made of cast-iron and wood ran along the entire facade. The rooms were large. The colourful crystal lamps that were either from Belgium or good copies of that style hung from high ceilings. However, the task of illuminating the room was entrusted to a fluorescent tube that plunged the room regularly into darkness due to a loose contact. The house was inhabited by an uncountable number of younger and older women as well as a few mostly younger men, who were always surrounded by feminine care, like the small boy sleeping in the living room on a bed under a mosquito net, his sleep protected by the grandmother on a second bed, who eyed us benignly after she had recovered from the initial surprise of our arrival. She sat upright, as if her backbone were made of cast iron, and she spoke only when she had to convey something important.

Her husband, the seventy-two-year-old patriarch, one of the zamindars of the town, knew only one topic: the grand heritage of the family. His grandfather had befriended the British district magistrate and had given him this house for a couple of years as his residence, after building it according to his own ideas, with many small and even smaller inner courtyards that led to rooms which nobody had ever counted. He must have owned more land than the patriarch today, who was left with a mere hundred acres that were, however, sufficient to lead a life on the veranda, to play host to the town and otherwise to look down on it. The land was still cultivated by tenant farmers who grew mostly rice. The earnings were divided fifty-fifty; the farmer had to pay for all expenses and investments, as the patriarch was quick to clarify, so that there could be no false impression that he did not earn enough from the deal. He was not happy with the farmers, probably because he thought that they harvested too little.

But I never got to know the reasons because one of his sons returned home and, after the interruption of greetings and explanations, the conversation turned towards the stone quarry the son was managing, where the workers had to break stones to gravel with hammers through the heat of the day, earning Rs 80, hardly enough to buy half a kilogram of tea. Of course, the son did not mention this; he boasted of the cinema hall he had built with his siblings, an old project, for which the patriarch had laid the foundation stone. The patriarch had remained graciously silent for a while, but as soon as his son came to the end of his account, he took back the floor and started pontificating about the tribals who had taken too many liberties, which was not acceptable. Because of their incessant protests, the new state of Jharkhand, to which Sahibganj belonged, had been cut out of Bihar, but they continued to be in the minority. Nevertheless, they now enjoyed so many privileges that one gradually felt as if they were the rulers of the land and he could not tolerate that. Their utter shamelessness was evident in the reservation quotas they demanded: 70 per cent of all government positions; this was not acceptable. His protest was cut short by a fit of coughing. As if on call, the patriarch's doctor made his grand entrance in the gathering of the joint family in the living room. After a few sentences, it was clear that he thought of himself as a buffoon. He imitated our Hindi accent and entangled us in a conversation of laid-out misunderstandings that inspired him to further jokes while he prepared the patriarch for an injection, which he finally pierced in the centre of his huge stomach.

The women had jointly cooked a wonderful supper of five vegetable dishes, rice, *puri*, dal, dahi and *Gulab Jamun* as dessert. A feast that we enjoyed on our own, the two of us on two small chairs behind two small tables facing the grandmother, who explained to us that according to old custom she had to ensure that we were well cared for. We enjoyed the delicious food while a happy Paras listed his favourites: *Men in Black*, Britney Spears, Arnold Schwarzenegger and Michael Jackson. When I mentioned that I preferred the music of the Santhals, I dropped considerably in his esteem. After dinner he requested us to sign his poetry album. We had to answer the printed questions: What was the happiest moment of your life? Who is your best friend? What is the meaning of friendship? What is your motto in life?

I realized that despite all its regal glory, the house lacked culture. There were no paintings or sculptures, even idols were few, besides the tiny family altar and the *Ganesh* in one of the courtyards that one of the girls had moulded from styrofoam for her aunt's wedding. There were no books, no musical instruments, no cassettes. Only one hobby was evident: Paras cultivated a small garden in a half-open corridor; there he grew the plants that he brought back every time he visited his parents in the village.

On the long and dark way to the hotel, we stopped at a pharmacy to buy adhesive plaster. A single candle lit the store. Suddenly the lights came on, and the chemist, a wiry Sikh, jumped up, clapped his hands and let out a jubilant shriek that was absorbed in other jubilant voices from all around. The chemist ran out into the street and started dancing. Then he remembered my presence and restrained himself.

'Three months,' he shouted. 'For three months we had no power!' A little further down the street, the transformer that had been repaired was already decorated with an opulent garland of the kind normally reserved for gods, saints, gurus or politicians. When we reached the hotel Paras had recommended, the manager justified the dirty, untidy room by pointing out that we were in Bihar, in Lalooland, and he grinned blissfully as if this absolved him once and for all of any personal responsibility.

Early next morning there was a knock on our door—I ignored it. The knocking grew into a drumming and I roused myself to a sleepy 'No'. But the drumming

226

continued. I jumped out of bed and pulled the door open. A slight young man stood outside and asked, with all the charm and politeness in the world, whether we would like some tea—I had to swallow my anger. Hardly had I dozed off when I was stirred by a further, equally insistent, round of hammering on the door. Another slight young man, keen to offer his services: he proposed a massage. Shortly thereafter there came further knocking on our door: another slight young man held a sheet of paper under my nose that had to be filled out immediately—arriving late at night, we had forgotten all about the police registration. We packed the rest of our sleep into our backpacks, paid the bill and stepped outside, where we heard that the tribals had announced a general strike. At the nearby *ghat*—where the electronically enhanced voice of a *pujari* recited passages from the *Ramayana*—we stumbled upon Paras and his cousin.

Paras claimed that the strike had to do with a bridge that was supposed to be built across the Ganges, but his cousin contradicted him: it was merely a political agitation.

'Oh yes, they demand this and that,' Paras said with conviction.

'Who are they?' I asked.

'The political forces!'

'Which political forces?'

'Those in power.'

Paras wasn't quite sure which party ruled Jharkhand, but one thing he knew for certain: the problems in Bihar and Jharkhand owed their existence to Laloo *Prasad* Yadav. Now that Jharkhand had been separated from Bihar, everything would improve.

At eight o'clock in the morning, St. Xavier's College was still quite empty. Walking down the long drive to the main building, I was reminded of the similarly well-maintained and beautiful grounds of Kenton College (the school of my early youth) in Kenya, another educational oasis from colonial times, defined by the St. James Bible and a geometrical understanding of gardening. In one of the rear wings, the teachers were lodged in rooms as small as cells. Father Anthony's door was ajar; he was sitting at his desk, correcting essays. He squinted heavily through one eye, the other he kept closed. But he still gave the impression of not missing anything. He was Maltese, from a simple and religious family; six of his eight brothers had become Jesuits like him. He was sent to India a few years after Independence, thanks to the administrative quirk by which the Jesuits in Malta fell under the purview of Sicily, and Sicily was responsible for India. For several decades he worked among the Santhals, the largest tribal community in the region with six million members. He had learnt Hindi and then Santhali, a beautiful language, he said, that was spoken perfectly even by the ten-year-olds. The younger generation of Santhals that had gone to school or even studied at a college had meanwhile been integrated into Indian society; there were more and more professionally successful Santhals, such as, for instance, the manager of the State Bank in Sahibganj.

But these people only went back to their villages for the occasional festival; they were urbanized and had already forgotten their roots. Father Anthony gave a glorious account of Santhal culture, but he spoke of the children having to be 'civilized' in schools.

Every five years he was allowed to travel home; he was due to go next year. The last time he was in Malta he had had to undergo open heart surgery—he lifted his shirt and showed us a scar that started at the throat and reached right down to the navel and laughed. 'Open heart surgery' seemed to be a joke that exacted laughter, so we obliged. Our conversation was interrupted by telephone calls from worried mothers inquiring whether school would go on despite the general strike. After about twenty calls, each one answered by Father Anthony with a resounding 'I don't know', his patience was exhausted. He laid the receiver across the cradle and smiled cunningly. We could continue our conversation in peace. The previous evening, he said, rickshaws with loudspeakers had ranged the streets, announcing that all shops had to remain closed the following day. The tribals, along with the scheduled castes, were demanding higher reservation quotas in the administrative and education system of the new state. Jharkhand was the result of a long-drawn battle of the tribals for self-determination. They had revolted against the British for the first time in 1831, and again in 1895. Quite a number of Santhals had been involved in the guerrilla movement of the *Naxalites* since the 1970s.

The principal stormed into the room and implored Father Anthony to replace the receiver on the cradle, as he himself was swamped with calls by nervous parents. Father Anthony complied with an innocent face, and our conversation suffered regular interruption again.

'How does a Catholic missionary school cope, deep in the backwoods of India?' I asked. 'How does it interact with the authorities?'

'No problem,' said Father Anthony, 'as long as we admit the scions of the local elite and pass them through. But as soon as we are forced to reject one of those children because he or she is not capable of following the lessons in English or is simply too old, there is immediate retaliation. If the father works for the municipal council, the school is burdened with injunctions. All of a sudden it is found that the school wall encroaches on the road, so we are ordered to pull down the wall and rebuild it a yard further back. If the father is a big shot at the telephone exchange, we suffer crossed connections or the lines go dead. If the concerned father holds a high position in the electricity department, our power supply is cut off, and it takes days to locate the fault. And if the parent is a high-ranking police officer, then a complaint is fabricated and one of our teachers or employees arrested and thrown into jail.

'We should actually introduce a separate class for compulsory students, 'the class of the select few. Otherwise there are few problems in this area. If you sit down for a cup of tea with the *Hindutva* people, they smile at you nicely and behave in a remarkably friendly and even charming way. But publicly they make hate speeches.'

He would suffer everything that came his way, Father Anthony said with complete detachment, and if he were summoned to burn, then he would burn, and with all the fat in his body he would burn well.

All other schools, one of the phone calls revealed, had closed, but the principal of St. Xavier's College, with its three thousand students, by far the most important educational institution in town, had decided to defy the strike. He was in touch with the police commissioner (whose son's studies must have been progressing well) who had assured him that the classes could go on without anxiety. However, nobody knew how the children were to come to school. The rickshaw drivers would not risk driving on the road, and private cars were in danger of being attacked. Past experiences made everybody in the teachers' common room fear an escalation. One of the teachers arrived in a huff and spoke of five hundred activists who had assembled at the gate to force the school to close.

But there were hardly fifty people gathered in front of the gate, and only ten of them were shouting slogans. There was an air of operetta to the *adivasi* protest. Another group of activists, around a hundred young men armed with hockey sticks, came along the way. One of them stopped beside me.

'Where to?'

'I am going for a walk.'

'Walk? How come?'

'Oh, just like that. And what are you doing?'

233

'We want to close the school.'

'Why?'

'We want more reserved seats for the tribals.'

'For that you need to close the school?'

The man took a deep breath and finally said with a note of rejection, 'I cannot explain to you.'

Bengal without a view

Bengal is one of *Ganga*'s children. Just as *Parvati* formed *Ganesh* from her own scurf, *Ganga* has formed the plains of Bengal from her own sediments. The river has carried ton by ton downwards and lifted the land out of the ocean. And she continues with her work: satellite pictures show a twelve thousand square metre peninsula being reclaimed from the Bay of Bengal. *Ganga* has made humanity the gift of the Sunderbans, an amphibian world between fresh and saline water; she allows the jute to prosper on the marshy soil of the delta, jute that the children harvest while swimming and lay out to dry on the bridges in flat sheaves. Later the jute is bundled along the roadside and exported in large quantities. But this gift has also been a curse to Bengal. The sediments block the canals and change the direction of the river. In the plains of Bengal—two hundred and fifty kilometres away from the coast, they lie a mere twenty metres above sea-level—the munificence of the river leads to devastating floods. The oldest existing Bengali text warns of the dangers of flooding and advises the people to stock up food. Since then the flooding has become more frequent, due to the massive deforestation in the Himalayas, and its effects even more horrifying.

~

I will always remember Behrampur as the Bengali town where I spent a hot and humid day at the landing place of a ferry that criss-crossed the Bhagirathi (as the Ganges is named once again), waiting for a boatman. After its change of name, the Ganges resembled a well-behaved canal, an exemplary protégée of irrigation. The course of the river seemed straightened, the mud embankments were fortified with concrete nets. It shouldn't be that difficult, we thought, to hire a boat to take us downstream to Katwa or Nabadwip, at distances of fifty and eighty kilometres respectively. The first boat owners we approached did not understand us, showed no interest or demanded too much money. But, at the landing place, we came across a mercurial figure who possessed boat, outboard motor and enterprising spirit, and who demanded a price that we could afford and he could profit from. We soon reached an agreement. He requested one hour's time to go home, pack a few belongings and say goodbye to his family. We decided that I would wait at the landing place while Pac would fetch the backpacks from the hotel and wait for us at a more convenient landing point further down the river.

I sat for a while in the shade and watched the passengers paying for the ferry, fishing coins out of every pocket and fold in their clothing. Then I went for a walk through the neighbourhood. This side of the river, Behrampur was a typical small town in India, a village breaking out of its limitations: on the box-shaped buildings and garage-like workshops stood enthroned billboards adorned with elegant trademarks, designed in the air-conditioned ad agencies

236

of Mumbai or Kolkata, and on the façades ran the stereotypical promises of telecommunication, offering cheap local calls as well as international connections. The localness found its sole expression in the use of the Bengali alphabet.

The rooftops served as a foundation for higher aspirations, the extensions often only half complete, waiting in frustration for reality to catch up with them. Nature was a guest that had outstayed its welcome and was no longer paid any attention. When it got too bothersome, it was cut down and thrown with its roots protruding into the road.

There was of course a small temple fastened to a banyan tree, a dry and shady place, an altar to indolence. I ordered a *chai* from one of the makeshift restaurants and sat outside sipping it, before I hurried back to the landing place and sat down again in the shade. Mentally prepared for a long wait, I had carried a book with me, a historical study of the long-drawn-out Bengali uprising against the British East India Company after the famine of 1770 that had inspired the construction of the egg-shaped silo in Patna.

In the course of this uprising, sadhus and fakirs had not only arrived at a strategic alliance but had fought side by side. There had been practically no harvest in the years 1769 and 1770; one-third of the population died, which meant just under ten million victims. The administration aggravated the crisis by allowing its officials to speculate with the scant rice reserves, to halt boats from other provinces on the Ganges and to plunder them. It was a point of honour for the distinguished British civil servants of the time to amass personal wealth beyond measure (the topos of Oriental corruption is a persistent myth, but as decadent as the Moghuls might have been, the corruption under their rule fell far short of genocide). Famished, desperate peasants swelled the ranks of the sadhus and fakirs; at the peak of the uprising, approximately fifty thousand holy men had taken to arms. In the worst year, the East India Company waived only 5 per cent of the land tax; in the subsequent year, it managed to increase its earnings by 10 per cent.

This was at a cost to many of the sadhus who were traders and possessed land that they had once acquired as remuneration for mercenary activities. From the neighbouring town of Murshidabad they had shipped silk, cloth, copper and spices up the Ganges all the way to Varanasi, from where the goods were transported further into the Deccan.

After more than an hour, I tried to find the whereabouts of the boatman. In vain. I was helpless against the heavy outpouring of Bengali. Through gestures, I indicated to the young men collecting the ferry toll that I would go for a shave; should the boatman arrive in the next ten minutes, he should please wait for me. But the boatman kept me waiting still; I took further comfort in my book, which cited the Bengali folk epic *Hakikat* and its portrait of the revolutionary Majnu Shah:

> *Majnu responded, he travelled*
> *far and wide.*
> *He heard the laments, he saw the hunger,*
> *and his heart lamented and suffered hunger.*
> *Peasants were reduced to beggars,*
> *mothers sold their children away.*

Wives and cattle were sold,
and those still alive
fed off corpses.
To one old pir Majnu narrated
the misery that had never left him.
The old man cried with rage and anguish,
and then gave the call:
Take up arms,
unite with the naga sadhus
raid the warehouse where rice is hoarded.
Distribute the food among the suffering
and drive them away, those Englishmen,
because we have no other choice.
Thousands of fakirs followed this call
all united behind their leader.
Even the sadhus congregated
and joined them as brothers.
Together they stormed and plundered
the kutcheries and the kothis of the Company.
The English were helpless, full of fear.
But for the peasants, this was encouragement
that their suffering would soon find an end.

In the meantime I had become an accepted feature of the landing place. Every half an hour the cashier sent a few henchmen to fetch me a *chai* or a soft drink; in exchange I shared my cigarettes with him. We had everything that we needed for the moment except a common language. Girls in white saris with red borders returned home from school, coolies carried on with their work, otherwise there was no indication why around fifty people wanted to cross the river every ten minutes.

An official on a massive motorcycle roared in, took note of me and asked what my problem was, which I explained to him with as much detail as irritation. He barked at a few people around and promised immediate clarification. He whizzed away, never to be seen again. The cashier asked another passenger who turned to me and explained with a gesture that the boatman was eating. That made sense. He must have had to wait till his wife had finished cooking lunch. Fair enough, I thought, we would be travelling down the Ganges with a sated boatman in a good mood. I gesticulated that I would also go for a bite and I stepped into the restaurant facing the barber's shop where I tried a vegetable hot-pot and stowed away a few chapattis.

At the landing place, only my book awaited me. The revolutionaries had plundered the British treasure chests. For years they controlled large parts of Bengal, skilfully avoiding any direct confrontation with the British troops, relying on guerrilla tactics. But ten years after the outbreak of the uprising, the first rifts in the coalition appeared. There were frequent internal disputes and conflicts. The sadhus and fakirs had no intention of transforming the victorious struggle into a sustainable system. The Company succeeded in isolating the rebels—militarily and economically— until the uprising fizzled out in around 1800. But the achievement of revolutionaries such as Majnu Shah was a glorious one in Indian history. Following in the foot-steps of leaders like Kabir, Guru Nanak and Pranami, they had united Hindus and Muslims into a loose federation with such strong integrative tendencies that groups from different cultural and social backgrounds joined hands to fight a common enemy—a common

242

front more inclusive than during the Indian struggle for independence a hundred years later!

I finished reading my book but there was still no sign of the boatman. I tried to extract some information from other ferrymen, but with no success. The afternoon was well established, many hours had passed since the boatman had taken leave of us. Pac waited on the other bank. Several times I was on the verge of taking a ferry and crossing over to the other side but each time I felt that the boatman would soon appear. I paced up and down, observed how the passengers boarded the ferry, placed bets against myself about which side of the ferry they would select. I lit the last cigarette that I would smoke in this place and crumpled the packet. A well-dressed man got off the ferry and asked me in good English what I was hoping to achieve by standing there. He listened to the loiterers filling in my story, then he shook his head firmly, 'You are wasting your time. You will not be able to travel any further by boat. For one thing, the current is too strong; besides, the stretch from here to Katwa is infested with

Naxalites. In this season no boatman will risk such a dangerous journey.'

'But how come nobody told me this,' I stammered, 'not one of all these people?'

'I excuse myself on behalf of my countrymen,' the man said.

'Sorry,' the loiterers mumbled.

'Why didn't you tell me?' I shouted. Then I jumped aboard the ferry; crossing, still angry, I could only stare into the unfathomable river.

In search of water supply

On every door of every room in the municipal council of Kolkata, a colossal institution of colonial provenance, there was pasted a note saying 'No Enquiry', usually in the standard size of a computer printout, which made it unmistakably clear to people such as myself that they and their questions were not welcome here. The guard at the main gate had sent me up to the second floor, and I had walked up and down this second floor several times, studying each and every note, some handwritten, some torn apart by hand, until I had discovered the legal, the health and the drainage departments, but I still had not found any reference to the department of water supply, which left me with no choice but to ask someone who appeared suitably omniscient. At that moment a well-dressed, energetic man passed by; he directed me without hesitation one floor downstairs, and I would have walked down the broad staircase if he hadn't mentioned in parting, 'Second floor'.

'On which floor are we?' I asked around among the waiting petitioners: sometimes I was told 'third', sometimes 'second'. I moved towards the balustrade, looked down and counted the floors, and despite my dedicated efforts at discovering a mezzanine floor or a landing that I may have missed, I could count only and exactly two floors. Another informant sent me down another corridor, with the instruction that I was to turn right at the end, where I encountered two guards chatting away with one other, these gentlemen initiating me into the mysterious classification by which 'water supply' fell under 'drainage'. Next to them, in one of the corners of this vast building, simple food was sold for a few rupees on leaf plates, a combination of rice and vegetables that was consumed by the petitioners as they squatted on the floor. At 'drainage' I found out that 'water supply' was located on the first floor; I walked down the stairs and along the corridors until I found the 'water supply' department, but the first officer seated behind the swing door informed me that the office of Mr Chatterjee, with whom I had an appointment, would be found on the second floor, to which I retorted that if he was actually working on the second floor then he was not to be found there. In a rare gesture of compassion, the officer decided to guide me there personally. At the end of the main corridor of the second floor, with which, by now, I was intimately familiar, there opened a narrow, shoulder-wide passage that I had mistaken for an emergency exit but which apparently led to Mr Chatterjee's sanctum, past a lift shaft, then a right turn, then a left turn, and down a few narrow passages, to an annexe of the building where the heads of the municipal council were accommodated, as it became clear to me when I suddenly found myself in front of the mayor's door. On the other side of the building were the offices of the corporators; my guide had to search for a while until he found the note with the printed letters 'water supply', at which he left me to my own devices, shaking off my heartfelt thanks as though they were a burden. I pushed open a glass door that wished me a Happy New Year 1999 and unexpectedly stood before a well-informed and confident secretary who invited me to enter the office of the corporator Sovan Chatterjee, where I was received by the board: 'If I was organized, I'd be dangerous'.

Apparently I had nothing to fear, for the corporator, a member of the mayor-in-council responsible for the water supply of Kolkata, had not turned up for our appointment. His reception room was lined with about thirty chairs, as though he were a man of lectures and recitations. The walls were adorned with an aged map and a few photographs showing a pumping station built in 1864 for the British army headquarters. Otherwise the room was empty and silent, a classical contrast to the loud corridors outside, full of tense, harried, lethargic people who were commandeered around, if anyone paid any attention to them at all. A similarly large adjacent room housed two smiling officials who puffed thoughtfully at their cigarettes. One of them informed me that Mr Chatterjee had been called away on an urgent matter, much regretted, an unforeseen emergency. I spent the next fifteen minutes imagining unforeseen emergencies in the field of water supply. After I had waited for half an hour in the office of the absent corporator, his secretary, a historian, decided on a makeshift solution and led me to the office of the chief water engineer, a long and winding journey back that I would have never completed on my own.

The chief water engineer, a papery person called Roy Chowdhary, demonstrated the utter unimportance of my person as well as his anger at the decision of the corporator to burden him with this appointment by having me sit at his desk directly to his left in the presence of incomprehensible negotiations and keeping me waiting for another half hour without even offering me a glass of water. When he finally turned towards me and we introduced ourselves, he rang for his secretary and asked him to staple a visiting card on to a two-page letter, a meticulous process that claimed the entire attention of the chief water engineer of the city of Kolkata as he stared, as if hypnotised, at the folding and stapling hands of his subordinate. Finally liberated from this task, he informed me that he had no time for me—the phone rang, and he smiled like a seer whose pessimistic prediction had once again been reaffirmed by destiny. He spoke for a long while in Bengali, drumming on the desk with his ballpoint pen, the secretary frozen in a stance awaiting orders. 'You can see for yourself how busy we are,' the chief water engineer said, as soon as he had replaced the receiver on to the cradle of one of the three telephones surrounding him. 'But you can send me an email and I will answer all your questions.'

Since this seemed as probable as a joint venture between the municipal council of Kolkata and McKinsey, I requested him in a most humble tone for permission to ask one or two quick and completely innocent questions so that I could see and understand more along the Bhagirathi during my next few days in Kolkata.

'Of course,' said the man in a charming tone, 'but please, would you like to drink something,' and he sent his secretary off on an errand.

'It still holds true,' he confirmed in reply to my first question, 'that the water supply of Kolkata, a city of twelve million inhabitants, is totally dependent on the river, also called the Bhagirathi, as you certainly know, and actually a part of the Ganges. There are a few bore-holes, but geologically the water that is pumped up is also Ganges water. However, the increasing salination causes a lot of headaches to the engineers and due to the highly irregular water level not all pumps can be operated during the dry season, which has a bad effect on the available water quantity. Further, there is a continuous struggle against bacterial pollution, thanks mainly to a very harmful fertilizer factory. Furthermore, at the start of the monsoon, the plankton levels are above the permissible limits.'

But despite all this, the municipal council had full control of the water supply, and I, who had travelled down the entire length of the river, could certainly understand what it meant that one of the largest cities in the world was dependent for survival on a river as moody and as ill-treated as the Ganges. Now he really had to get back to his work, he excused himself, but maybe I could explain before leaving why I was planning to write a book on the Ganges.

Farewell without end

In Diamond Harbour (a name that is explained by the sunset) the river smelt like the sea. On the opposite bank, the fires of the refineries of Haldia, a modern port that was built in 1977 to reduce the burden on the increasingly overloaded port of Kolkata, were burning. Diamond Harbour was lined by a beautiful promenade but nobody went for a walk. A lone ice-cream vendor slowly made his rounds like the last functioning part of a toy whose batteries were running out. A few ships were docked because of the low tide.

We reached the main street of Diamond Harbour and took pleasure in small things. A vendor had arranged bananas to form a huge lotus.

'If I buy a few of your bananas,' I said to him, 'I would damage the picture.'

'If you buy some,' he said to me, 'I can form a new picture tomorrow.'

Behind the chain-smoking buses that declared their haste to the passengers, a *chai-wallah* prepared tea with the flair, the gestures and the gusto of an eccentric barman. He was happy to offer us two cups of *chai*. Otherwise the outlook was as flat as the afternoon light and the land between Diamond Harbour and the Bay of Bengal.

~

Cows meant wealth, horses symbolized power. Cows were a part of everyday life while horses, few in number and imported from the border lands in the northwest, guaranteed might. On special occasions, when the king wished to declare his supremacy, a horse was sacrificed in a bloody ritual called the Ashvamedha. Sometimes a greedy worldly ruler competed with the gods. When King Sagara of the Solar dynasty of Ayodhya planned a ritual whose magnitude surprised no one since he had already procreated sixty thousand sons, Indra—disguised as a demon—stole the sacrificial horse. The king sent out his sons to bring back the horse, for the equilibrium of the kingdom was at stake. The sons searched far and wide, in the upper and in the lower worlds. Finally they saw the horse grazing peacefully on a meadow near the hermitage of Kapil Muni, whom they immediately accused of being the thief. Kapil Muni tried to explain to them that he had not stolen the horse, he had not lured it away nor had he used any force. He had let the horse be, just as he let all things be. But the royal sons, unused to being corrected in their judgement, drew their swords and fell upon him. It was an uneven fight. Kapil Muni hurled a wrathful curse at them, which set the hair of the warriors ablaze. They burned and burned, until all that was left of the royal sons was a mountain of ashes.

In the palace the king was tyrannized by his impatience. First someone had stolen his horse, now his sixty thousand sons had vanished from the face of the earth. He sent out his grandson Anshuman. After a long journey, Anshuman reached the abode of Kapil Muni who told him what had happened and informed him that the final rites could only be completed with the water of the heavenly *Ganga*, for it was a serious sin to insult a *rishi*. The royal sons would be freed of their sins only when their ashes were accepted by the waters of the *Ganga*.

It took the Solar dynasty three generations to bring forth someone capable of bringing *Ganga* down from the heavens. His name was Bhagiratha. Over a thousand years of penance, he collected so much *tapas* that *Brahma* appeared before him and warned him against bringing *Ganga*, flowing through heaven as the milky way, down to earth. The masses of water would crush the earth. *Shiva* alone was capable of softening the impact. Bhagiratha appealed to *Shiva*: at Mount *Kailash* he waited for him for a whole year, standing only on his big toe. Impressed, *Shiva* promised him help. When *Ganga* burst from the heavens, he broke her fall with his entangled hair and let the water flow in long streams down to earth. Bhagiratha rode in front, *Ganga* followed him. They reached the spot where the dead ancestors lay. *Ganga* flowed over the ashes and took them in. The souls of the sixty thousand warriors were at peace; *Ganga* relaxed and spread out into an ocean.

We were standing exactly at that spot, before us the Kapil Muni temple, a simple structure that housed three nearly formless idols: *Ganga* on the left, Bhagiratha in the centre, Kapil Muni to the right. Five hundred and one electricity poles were rammed into the ground in tidy rows in the vast free space in front of the temple, a parade waiting for the mela that takes place in mid-January when half a million pilgrims are given another chance to wash their sins away. (The equations must match: To cleanse herself of all these sins, *Ganga* visits a shrine in southern India, in summer, when the gods are sleeping.)

On this island in the delta, the shark, and not the crocodile, is *Ganga*'s *vahana*. In earlier days some pilgrims waded into the sea after a last *puja*, hoping for shark and salvation. But there were too many pilgrims and the sharks were often full—not every sacrifice was accepted by the predators. The pilgrims perceived their survival as a bad omen; they went back to the shore, confused and convinced that their sacrifice had been refused because of the weight of their sins.

~

At sunset we sat on the long beach, next to the natural port formed by a channel behind a sand dune. Boats overburdened with fishermen put out to sea; red crabs crawled out of their holes and ran across the bright sand, thousands of them. Each crab seemed to invent a new direction, scuttling briskly from hole to hole. When we approached them, the crabs vanished, and the beach appeared empty, as if we had only dreamt of the red creatures. As soon as we sat down and peace took hold of us, they came out again and crept over the sand, as if four headless servants with bony legs were carrying a palanquin.

The sun was nearly gone when we noticed a *sadhu* slowly approaching. He stopped in front of us, an emaciated body covered with the skin of an old elephant, and asked for alms. We offered him a few coins, and he spoke a mantra; then he sat down next to us and asked where our journey was taking us.

'Our journey has come to an end.'

'*Ganga* ka *yatra*?'

'Yes.'

'You are blessed.'

'We are sad.'

'Why sad?'

'Because our journey has come to an end.'

The old *sadhu* laughed.

'You have memories. Real and not so real, like the journey itself.'

He grabbed my wrist and pressed it so hard that it hurt.

'I will tell you something. A man sits by the bed of his son. The son is dying. The man falls asleep; he dreams he has fifteen sons, handsome, intelligent, strong sons, who grow up and make him happy. His wife wakes him up. "How can you sleep? Our son is dead and you are sleeping. Are you not sad?"

'"Sad about whom?" the man said. "The fifteen sons that I shall forget because you woke me up, or the son we have lost today, who will not remain in my memory when I am dead."'

The *sadhu* laughed and looked at us, he coughed and laughed again as he stood up, coughed, laughed when he turned around, coughed, shook with laughter as he went away, as slowly as he had come. Soon he was a silhouette on the grey beach, under a sky wearing washed-out saris. He disappeared among some boys, a few of them playing cricket, others playing football.

Thick clouds piled up on the horizon, as if the sun had fallen into the sea with a splash. The waves were no longer visible. We heard them roll over in breakers, before falling silent, just like *Ganga* dissolved into further immensity.

Acknowledgements

Without Katrin the journey would have been half as inspirational.

Without Krish the writing would have taken twice as long.

Without Ranjit the translation would have been one-sided.

And special gratitude to all the people who helped us, led us and gave us shelter—especially Gopal and Rekha Sutwala for their hospitality in Kanpur, Arvind Parikh for the precious contacts with musicians along the way, Kiran Wagle and Taj Hotels for asylums of comfort, Karl Dantas for all the support systems, Raj Singh for his interest and practical help, Peter Pannke and Markus Wieser for an encouraging early reading of the German manuscript, Murray McCartney for a very precise and incorruptible reading of the English translation, and all the wonderful professionals at Hanser Verlag, Penguin Books India, and Haus Publishing.

The poems on pages 158/9, 172/3, 175/6, are quoted from 'The Bijak of Kabir', translated by Linda Hess and Shukdeo Singh (Oxford, 2002).

Glossary

Aarti	Evening ritual
Adivasi	Indian indigenous tribes
Ahimsa	Non-violence
Arjuna	Central figure of the Mahabharata
Ashram	Name of any place, where spiritual people gather; normally refers to the Hindu equivalent of a retreat or hermitage
Avatar	Divine incarnation
Baba	Respectful address to a hermit
Bhagvan	God
Bhagavadgita	'The Song of God', educational poem
Bhajan	Worshipful and devoted singing
Bharat	India
BJP	Bharatiya Janata Party
Bol	Syllable of the Tabla language
Brahma	Within the holy Hindu trinity Brahma represents the divine power of creation
Chai	Tea, cooked with milk and sugar
Charpoy	Bed with a woven mattress
Chillum	(hashish) Pipe
Dacoit	Robber

Dalit	'The broken ones', the term which the outcastes or casteless give themselves
Damru	Drum of Shiva
Darshan	Blessing of sight and of being seen
Devganga	Second Ganga
Dharma	The inherent nature of a person or object, duty in life, order or law
Dhoti	Material, wrapped around the hips
Dhruv	Northern star
Diwali	Festival celebrated in October/November and marked by lighting of lamps and candles, feasting, and exchange of gifts
Dosa	Thin pancake (South India)
Durga Puja	Festival of the Goddess Durga, celebrated mainly in Bengal
Ganesh	Elephant-headed god, who removes all obstacles
Ganga	Name of the Goddess, in India also the name of the river Ganges
Gangajal	Blessed water of the Ganges
Ghat	Stairs, bathing spot on a river, lake or water pool
Ghee	Cleared butter
Gita	Song, also abbreviation of the Bhagavadgita
Gotra	Each Brahman belongs to a gotra, which goes back to a mystical rishi. Traditionally a Brahman from one gotra can only marry into another gotra.
Gulab Jamun	Dessert made from cooked milk
Guru	Spiritual teacher
Gurukul	Spiritual school
Halwa	Dessert

Hanuman	King of the Monkeys, ally of Rama (Ramayana)
Haridwar	City, 'the Gate of Vishnu'
Hindutva	Term for an extreme nationalist and intolerant version of Hinduism
Ishwar	'God of the Universe', the concept of the personification of a God as the Creator of the Universe
Jain	Follower of Jina, the 'Victor'; Jains believe that non-injury to living beings is the highest religion and their code of ethics is based on sympathy and compassion.
Kailash	Holy mountain in Tibet, the seat of the God Shiva
Kali	'The Black One', partner of Shiva, on the one hand the holy mother goddess and on the other hand representing the destructive powers
Kama	Lust, desire; the divine embodiment of this principle
Kashi	'City of Light', Varanasi
Kurta	Long dress worn by men, especially in northern India
Kusha	Holy grass; longish reed with a white blossom which flowers at the end of the monsoon and which is wound around the ring finger during the puja
Langoti	Long piece of cloth worn traditionally as undergarment
Lingam	Linga means sign and a lingam is the sign of the penis and as a fertility symbol represents the God Shiva

Lota	Small vessel used for rituals near the water
Mahabharata	'The Great Indian History', longest epic tale, originally told in Sanskrit
Mahatma	'Great Soul', holy man
Mandir	Temple
Moksha	Deliverance
Mrityu	Goddess of Death
Naga	Serpent
Namahashivay	Address to Shiva
Nandi	The bull, mount of God Shiva
Naxalites	Maoist rebels, who since 1967 are fighting against the 'semi-feudal and semi-colonial' structures in the countryside
NRI	Non-Resident-Indian
Om	Mystical sound, symbol of the essence of spiritual knowledge
Paan	Betel nut
Pandit	Master, wise man
Parishad	Council, congregation
Parvati	'Daughter of the Mountain', partner of God Shiva
Pranam	'Bow', respectful greeting
Prasad	Blessed by the gods, eaten by men
Puja	Ritual of worship
Pujari	Temple priest
Purana	'Old texts', Sanskrit texts about the myths and legends of creation, divine biographies and genealogies of holy men
Puri	Thin pasties
Raja	King
Ram	God
Rama	King, incarnation of God Vishnu

Ramayana	Classical Sanskrit epos
Ravana	In the Ramayana, the demon king of Sri Lanka
Rishi	Wise man, often possessing super-natural powers
Rishikesh	City: 'Hair of the Wise Men'
RJD	Rashtriya Janata Dal, national peoples movement
Roti	Flat bread
RSS	Rashtriya Swayamsevak Sangh, association of national self-help
Sadhu	Ascetic, often clothed in saffron-coloured wraps, who reach Sannyasi in early age. This last of the four stages of a typical Hindu life is normally reached only after the learning phase, the stage of the patriarch and then that of the elder. It is the most important stage and only if one leads an unblemished life during this final, fourth phase man can reach final salvation.
Sangam	Confluence
Sanskrit	Most important language of classical Indian literature
Sarpanch	Village elder
Shanti	Peace
Shiva	'The Kind, the Generous, the Gracious One', the great ascetic, destroyer of ignorance, worshipped by many as the all-powerful god
Sita	Wife of Rama
Skanda	Son of Shiva, also known as Saravanodbhava

Snaan	Ritual bath
Shurpanakha	In the Ramayana, the demonic and ugly sister of Ravana
Sufi	Islamic mystic. Sufism: 'To find joy in one's heart, when the time of sorrow is near.' (Rumi)
Susa	(also susu) Dolphin
Tabla	Double drum, important rhythmical instrument in classical Hindustani music
Tamasha	major commotion
Tapas	energy acquired through ascetic self-denial
Taraka	Powerful demon
Tata Sumo	Indian four-wheel drive
Upanishades	'to sit close to the teacher', philosophical texts also known as Vedanta
Valmiki	Mystical author of the Ramayana
Vibhuti	Blessed ash of burned cow dung
Vyasa	Mystical author of the Mahabharata
Wah	Expression of delight
Wallah	'belonging to', in the sense of 'working with' or 'dealing with'
Veda	'divine knowledge', the most sacred of the Hindu scriptures, hymns written in an old form of Sanskrit; the oldest may date from 1500 or 2000 BC
Yagna	Sacrificial ritual with fire
Yatra	Pilgrimage
Zamindar	Owner of the land